★★★ DOGS ★★★
WHO SERVE

ALSO BY LISA ROGAK

The True Tails of Baker and Taylor: The Library Cats Who Left Their Pawprints on a Small Town . . . and the World (with Ian Louch)

Cats on the Job: 50 Fabulous Felines Who Purr, Mouse, & Even Sing for Their Supper

Angry Optimist: The Life and Times of Jon Stewart

One Big Happy Family: Heartwarming Stories of Animals Caring for One Another

Dan Brown: The Unauthorized Biography

Dogs of Courage: The Heroism and Heart of Working Dogs Around the World

The Dogs of War: The Courage, Love, and Loyalty of Military Working Dogs

And Nothing but the Truthiness: The Rise (and Further Rise) of Stephen Colbert

Michelle Obama in Her Own Words: The Views and Values of America's First Lady

Barack Obama in His Own Words

Haunted Heart: The Life and Times of Stephen King

A Boy Named Shel: The Life and Times of Shel Silverstein

★★★ DOGS ★★★
WHO SERVE

INCREDIBLE STORIES OF OUR CANINE MILITARY HEROES

LISA ROGAK

THOMAS DUNNE BOOKS

ST. MARTIN'S GRIFFIN

NEW YORK

THOMAS DUNNE BOOKS.
An imprint of St. Martin's Press.

DOGS WHO SERVE. Copyright © 2016 by Fat Pencil LLC. All rights reserved. Printed in China. For information, address St. Martin's Press, 175 Fifth Avenue, New York, N.Y. 10010.

www.thomasdunnebooks.com
www.stmartins.com

Designed by Omar Chapa

The Library of Congress Cataloging-in-Publication Data is available upon request.

ISBN 978-1-250-08062-2 (trade paperback)
ISBN 978-1-4668-9254-5 (e-book)

Our books may be purchased in bulk for promotional, educational, or business use. Please contact your local bookseller or the Macmillan Corporate and Premium Sales Department at 1-800-221-7945, extension 5442, or by e-mail at MacmillanSpecialMarkets @macmillan.com.

First Edition: October 2016

10 9 8 7 6 5 4 3 2 1

For all of the military journalists, photographers, and Public Affairs staffers
who tell the stories of these brave canine soldiers and the men
and women who work alongside them

CONTENTS

★★★ DOGS ★★★

WHO SERVE

INTRODUCTION

Ever since May 2011, when the news first hit that there was a highly trained Belgian Malinois dog named Cairo who assisted a team of elite Navy SEALs in the raid that located and subsequently killed Osama bin Laden, people from all over have clamored for more information about the lives of the Military Working Dogs who serve in all branches of the U.S. military.

Though there have been countless stories and video news reports that have appeared in the years since the raid, people still can't get enough, whether it's learning about the lives of MWDs—short for "Military Working Dogs"—in wartime or the details about their constant training routines or what happens to them after they retire. Why do people love to hear stories about our canine soldiers? In short, because they represent everything that is great about the U.S. military. First of all, they serve a unique and specific purpose that no two-legged soldier could ever fill:

"These dogs act as a first line of defense against enemy threats because they can smell things and go places that humans can't," said Tech. Sgt. Roseann

Kelly, assistant flight chief with the 366th Security Forces Squadron at Mountain Home Air Force Base in Idaho.

Plus, their mere presence can have a huge effect even if they never bark or growl. "They're a force multiplier, they give more power than just people alone," said S.Sgt. Samuel Giordano, a handler at RAF Mildenhall in the United Kingdom. "The dogs are a huge psychological deterrent; people are often scared of them, and we use them for our own protection as well as force and resource protection."

Indeed, MWDs are often regarded as the last resort before a soldier decides to use deadly force. "When you fire a weapon, you can't take that bullet back," said Cpl. Ryan Pilz, a handler based at Marine Corps Base at Camp Lejeune, North Carolina. "These dogs are like our retractable bullets. A dog may chase after an enemy and attack him, but if the enemy surrenders or backs down, the dog can be called back."

But even though a canine soldier naturally serves as an effective weapon and crime deterrent, he needs a highly trained two-legged soldier to guide him.

"A dog team is a special kind of asset," said Lance Cpl. Pete Hernandez, a handler with the 3rd Marine Expeditionary Force based in Okinawa, Japan. "It relies on one handler building a bond with his partner. [Together] . . . they can pinpoint where an odor is, tell explosive ordnance disposal Marines where to search, and if that's not available we can choose an alternate route and not have to put [Marines] in danger. I would definitely say that I put my life in my dog's hands."

While the dog has the nose, the handler is responsible for interpreting and serving as translator for other humans; as such, most handlers would add Canine Mind Reading to the long list of skills that are necessary to serve as the human side of an effective MWD team. "You have to be able to read the dog's change in behavior and be able to control them," said S.Sgt. Randy Cottner, a military police dog handler. "I know he's going to get sick before he gets sick."

"While there are soldiers throughout the ranks that only see military working dogs as 'dogs,' you'd be hard-pressed to find a handler that feels this way," said Sgt. 1st Class Aaron Meier, kennel master with the 550th Military Working Dog Detachment at Fort Bragg, North Carolina. "They become close, sometimes to an extent that it seems that they are one entity. In the end,

a dog becomes an extension of the handler. Without one, the other is useless."

However, to develop that seamless connection, it usually requires weeks or months of long hours of training together and just hanging out. While some dogs and handlers instantly bond from the first moment of meeting, the reality is usually something different, and so the job of handler is not for the impatient.

"It took three to six months to develop the type of bond I wanted with Kiara," said S.Sgt. Rosanne Caballero, an MWD trainer with the 799th Security Forces Squadron at Creech Air Force Base in Nevada. "I spent a lot of time with her, got to know her, and she was with me everywhere I went while on duty. There's more to this job [than people see] and it's very time consuming. You have to want it. If your heart isn't set in it, then this job isn't for you."

As with any relationship that depends on being so closely attuned to your partner, trust is absolutely essential.

"If the dog cannot trust you or you cannot trust the dog, there cannot be a rapport established and you will never become a team," said S.Sgt. Nicholas Drake, an MWD trainer with the 354th Security Forces Squadron at Eielson Air Force Base in Alaska. "You will make mistakes and you have to be willing to let the dog make mistakes."

And the primary way they accomplish this trust is by letting a dog do dog things: walking around the base, jumping through the hoops and climbing ladders on the obstacle course, and chasing a ball or tugging on a rope for hours.

Both dog and human are obviously having a blast. But toss and fetch and the other games are actually bringing them together, to form a bond that will eventually help both to protect their fellow soldiers as well as each other when called upon to search for explosives and / or bad guys both at home and overseas.

"It looks like play time for the dog and in a sense it is," said Tech. Sgt. Matthew Mosher, a handler who is also based out of Eielson Air Force Base. "Everything needs to be fun for the dog . . . and positive."

Once an MWD team achieves that bond, well, it's hard to know where one begins and the other one starts; most MWDs are essentially a well-oiled machine where words are often not necessary.

"When you achieve that level of rapport there is nothing that dog won't do for you," said Mosher. "And once it's achieved, it's unbreakable."

At the same time, just like their human counterparts, canine soldiers each have their own distinctive personalities, and they can act differently with different people.

"Imagine your M-4 [rifle], and now imagine your M-4 can communicate with you, and has good and bad days and a personality," said Capt. Jake Porter, the provost marshal at Forward Operating Base Spin Boldak in Afghanistan. "That's what handlers have to be able to deal with."

In the years since my book *The Dogs of War: The Courage, Love, and Loyalty of Military Working Dogs* was published in the fall of 2011, it's clear that readers love to read about these incredible four-legged soldiers. Indeed, interspersed between the chapters where I covered training, equipment, and life on the front lines some of the most popular parts of *Dogs of War* were the individual profiles of the MWDs scattered throughout the book in sidebars: the story of Rex, an MWD who served in Vietnam who received two gold crowns from a regular dentist and was able to return to serve by his partner's side, and a German shepherd named Bodo, who saved his handler's life in Iraq by pulling him out of the line of gunfire.

In addition to the heartwarming stories of these canine soldiers in *The Dogs of War*, readers also marveled at the amazing photos that showed the dogs

lunging through the air, jumping out of perfectly good helicopters, and always, *always* displaying the devotion they feel for their human partners. The public affairs departments that are a crucial part of any military base at home and overseas love to do stories about the canine soldiers in their employ, and it definitely shows. From the photos of MWDs wearing goggles—aka Doggles— and booties to pictures showing them being hoisted out of helicopters and even jumping out of planes, it's these pictures that accurately and poignantly help capture the lives of these heroic dogs.

But there's a softer side, too, whether it's a picture of the Belgian Malinois

puppies who are specially bred and trained to serve and protect two-legged soldiers or one of the unguarded moments that shows a handler giving his canine
partner the last drops of water from a canteen on a 120-degrees-in-the-shade
day in a desert encampment; these photographs serve to reveal a little more

about these incredible partnerships.

And so *Dogs Who Serve* is devoted to telling the great stories of MWDs
and their handlers along with featuring amazing photos that show them both
at work and play. I hope that these stories and photos will help readers to appreciate and learn a little bit more about the absolute love and devotion that
these dogs show towards their jobs and human partners and that they serve
their country without question.

In the end, while life as a handler and MWD team certainly isn't easy, the
rewards are plentiful.

"It's great to come in to work and see your best friend every day," said Sgt. Joseph Nault, an MWD trainer at Creech Air Force Base in Nevada. "It doesn't matter if you're not having a good day; [the dogs are] . . . going to get you going."

"There is no better job in the Air Force. I put on my uniform and play with a dog," said S.Sgt. Christopher Michaud, Nault's co-worker at the 799th SFS and kennel master at the base. "What other job is like that where you get to go to work every day and get paid to play with dogs all day?"

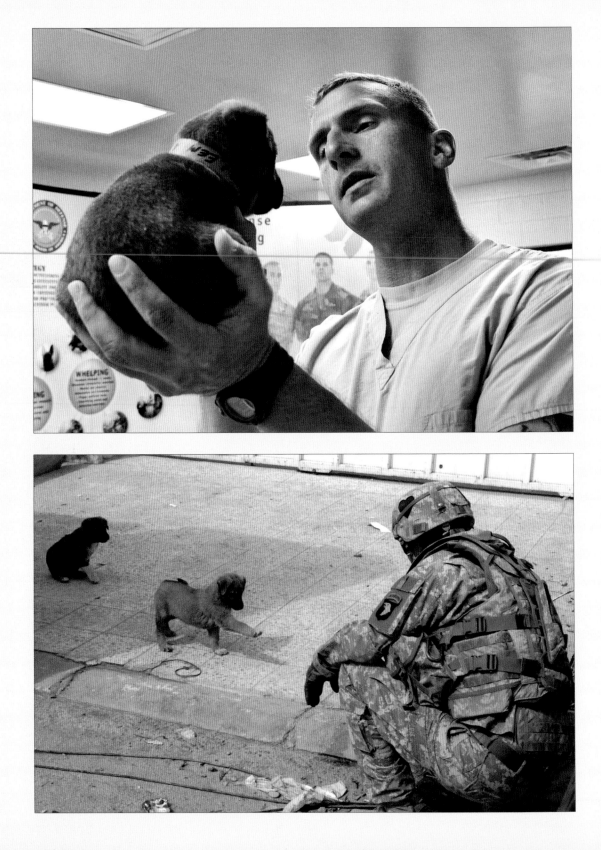

★★★ (1) ★★★
BASIC TRAINING

"They say not to get too attached to the dog you work with but how can you not get attached to something you work with for hours day in and day out?" asked Cpl. Darren Westmoreland, an MWD handler based at the Marine Corps Air Ground Combat Center in Twentynine Palms, California.

Especially when they're cute puppies?

Indeed, that's the most difficult part of working with an MWD, whether you're a handler teamed up with a canine partner for a two-year commitment or a trainer in charge of evaluating a bunch of squirming puppies to decide which one is going to head off to protect American soldiers put in harm's way.

But happily, there are many people who are willing to do it. After all, it's a fulfilling—and entertaining—way to serve their country.

THE YOUNGEST RECRUIT: DDONJA

It's a pretty fancy name for such a small, cute puppy: Donja, or Ddonja if you want to get technical.

All of the puppies born into the Military Working Dog Breeding Program at Lackland Air Force Base in San Antonio, Texas, are given names that begin with doubled letters to characterize the dogs as belonging to the program, where the aim is to supply MWDs to every branch of the U.S. military.

As such, it's one of the largest military breeding programs in the world.

At only eleven weeks of age, it's hard to believe that the wriggly Belgian Malinois with the enormous ears will develop into a highly trained ferocious warrior who will undoubtedly head off to a volatile part of the world, where her ultra-sensitive sense of smell will help save the lives of American soldiers.

Though the military has long acquired canine soldiers from a mix of private breeders, individuals, and even shelters, the focus in recent years has shifted to a desire for uniformity by working with a breed with a combination of

strength and temperament that will excel at whatever the military can throw at it. Defense experts determined that the Belgian Malinois was close to perfect for their needs due to the breed's adaptability and genetic ruggedness; German shepherds were previously the breed of choice, but many of the dogs tended to develop hip dysplasia in their later years, which is less likely to become a problem for Belgian Malinois.

This is where Ddonja comes in. "We can provide a product that's specially tailored for our needs," said Bernadine Green, deputy director of Lackland's breeding program. "We can start these puppies from birth and really start guiding them along the Department of Defense training path."

That path consists of several stages for future canine soldiers to graduate from: first up, the whelping stage, from birth through about two months old; next is living with a foster family, which is followed by basic training, which

focuses on obedience, and finally advanced training to teach patrol and detection skills. Then, if the dog completes all the required tests and certifications, the fledgling canine soldier is assigned to a military base where he is teamed up with the first of several two-legged partners to serve out his military career.

Throughout the entire process, trainers and civilians alike learn about a particular dog's strengths and weaknesses, which will help to determine whether a dog is trained to detect explosives or narcotics or, indeed, if the canine washes out of the program entirely.

During the first stage, staff at the breeding program are looking for a sense of each puppy's personality. As Green described it, a puppy who grows into a successful MWD should be "inquisitive, eager to check out new places, sociable, not overly aggressive, and eager to play with objects, such as toys and balls." Obviously, not being afraid of loud noises is a requirement.

As Ddonja chewed on a rope, batted at a ball, and tumbled around the floor with her littermates, she appeared more than ready for the next stage.

FOSTERING LOYALTY: BBELLA

When the Belgian Malinois puppies are about eight weeks old, they are placed in a foster home, where they stay for about five months to build socialization skills and learn basic obedience. Most of the foster families are volunteers who live in and around San Antonio and outlying communities. Some are service members or veterans, while others have a military affiliation, but all volunteer for the job because they share a common desire to serve.

"Families love to do it," said Bernadine Green. "It's their way of giving back to the community and the military, and also for the sheer pleasure of caring for a puppy."

Living in a foster home is an integral part of an MWD's development. "Families take them everywhere—to school, playgrounds, stores, work," said Green. "It broadens the puppy's

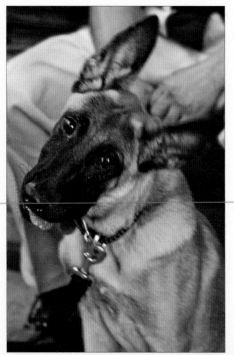

horizon. Without these foster parents raising puppies, we don't get well-rounded dogs." Tracy Cann, a foster consultant with the breeding program, concurs. "Working dogs are very high energy and intelligent and growing up in a kennel could make them shy and introverted when we need them to be just the opposite," she said. "Foster [families] . . . raise the puppies in their homes and socialize them in all kinds of environments, which would not be possible if they were raised in kennels."

When a Belgian Malinois puppy named Bbella, all paws and ears, came to live with Hector Hernandez and his family, they weren't sure what they were getting themselves into, which certainly went double for the family's resident dog, Rosie. But Hernandez, a Navy veteran and training instructor at the Naval Technical Training Center at Lackland, said that signing up for the foster program has provided him with a way where he can continue to serve his country.

"I miss the military," said Hernandez, who retired from the Navy in January 2011. "I feel like I have a lot of good fight in me. I want to serve further."

While the day-to-day life of living with a foster puppy can be a lot of fun mixed with an occasional dose of frustration, the truth is that the end of the period is never far from the minds of the families.

"We have a lady who's fostered 13 puppies for us," said Green, adding that when the time comes for a puppy to return to Lackland, "she cries a blue streak."

BASIC TRAINING

After the foster period ends, the puppies—who, at around seven months of age, are now officially adolescents—head back to Lackland for what is essentially basic training for canines. They'll spend the first couple of weeks settling into life in a kennel at the base, which admittedly can be a rough adjustment to make after living in the relative cushiness of a family home, complete with comfortable furniture and at least several family members spoiling the puppy for the majority of her waking hours.

Indeed, though the kennel staff obviously take excellent care of the young pups upon their return to Lackland, some of the dogs become visibly depressed from losing their home and foster families, as well as sleeping in the comparatively harsh environment of a kennel. If the depression continues for more than a few weeks, staff take it as a clear sign that the puppy will not be able to deal with the rigors and uncertainties of military life. At this point the puppy will be put up for adoption and go to live with either the foster family or an active-duty service member or civilian employee at the base. More often than not, there's a lengthy waiting list of people who would love to welcome the puppy into their homes.

Those canines who remain then begin a five-month program of training and tests designed to analyze a dog's strengths as well as his weaknesses. Anything and anyone a dog may encounter on a military base or in a war zone comes into play to further weed out those canines who may not be suitable for a lifetime career as an MWD. Gunfire, bombed-out buildings in a harsh desert environment, and helicopter landings and takeoffs are all part of the program.

Trainers are also watching to see if a dog prefers to spend more of her time biting and chewing on a ball or rag even if an unfamiliar and enticing aroma wafts by or will relinquish the ball and veer off in the direction of the scent, curious to follow where it leads.

Dogs who favor the ball are more likely to excel as patrol dogs, tasked with protecting a military base from potential criminals, while the dog who was distracted by the scent will probably develop into a fine detection dog, specializing in searching for either explosives or narcotics. In recent years, however, the military has branched out into training and certifying MWDs in both detection and patrol—known as dual-purpose dogs—in order to put the dog to full use.

"Right now, the need is great for detection dogs," said Green. "These puppies will save more people with their nose than they ever will with their teeth."

ADVANCED TRAINING

When the dogs graduate from basic training, they head directly into a two-month intensive program at Lackland known as DTS training, short for the Dog Training Section. As before, after some time is allowed for the adjustment from one program to the next they head directly into a regimen of exercises and training sessions where a variety of different handlers will put them through their paces.

By the time dogs make it into the DTS program—which consists of one month of patrol work and one month of detection training—the job of their trainers and handlers is to build the finest canine soldiers they can manage. "I compare it to coaching Barry Sanders' or Michael Jordan's son," trainer S.Sgt. Victor Nelson said. "It's just a matter of guiding them along the path. As far as genetics and talent, they already have it."

"In my world, you don't want a dog you have to coax to do anything," said Bernadine Green. "You want a dog that comes right out of the gate and says,

"'Let's go to work.'"

But as is the case in life, nothing is ever guaranteed. Upon watching a group of trainers put several dogs through their paces on the training course, Dr. Stewart Hilliard, logistics chief with Lackland's breeding program, marveled how even if a previous pairing produced a litter of pups where seven out of eight went on to become hardworking canine soldiers, just repeating the bloodline doesn't mean that lightning will strike twice. In fact, it's highly unlikely.

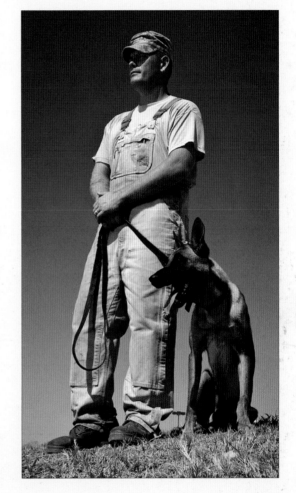

"One of the interesting things about breeding is there are no guarantees," he said. "Even if we've had a very successful breeding of a particular male and female, if we repeat the breeding there is no guarantee the result is going to be as good as the first time. This shows you that genetics are highly variable, that environment plays a big role, and it is very subtle interactions between genetics and environment that lead to good working dogs."

After the program ends, each dog is again tested, and if he passes with flying colors he is certified and assigned to a military base or post to begin what will hopefully turn out to be a long and illustrious career.

SERGEANT GRECO, REPORTING FOR DUTY, SIR!

When a new canine recruit by the name of Greco arrived at Joint Base Lewis-

McChord in Washington State in the summer of 2015, neither he nor his new handler, Army S.Sgt. Adam Serella with the 95th Military Police Detachment, knew exactly what to expect. While Serella was an experienced trainer and handler, every dog is different; in addition, the stress of travel and arrival on a new base, as well as some uncertainty about what came next, can mask a dog's personality until he settles in.

But first things first: the new soldier needed a bath. "He smelled pretty bad, so I put him in the tub and gave him his toy to chew on," Serella said. "He just had this sad *Why are you doing this?* look on his face."

After a vigorous towel drying, Serella and Greco dove right into getting acquainted with each other through playing together and going on walks. Serella also checked in on his new partner's obedience skills. They were able to concentrate since there are few distractions both inside the kennel and outside on the training fields. "Unlike dogs at home, these dogs don't have toys laying

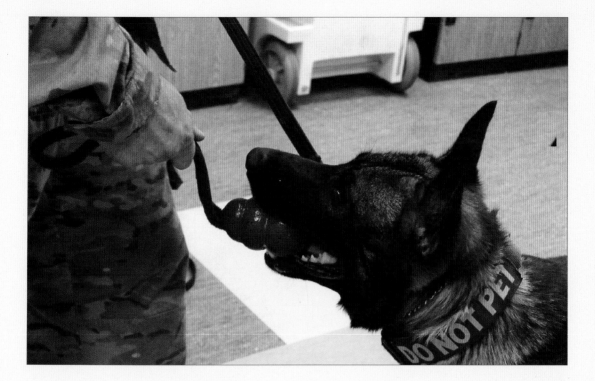

around, so all the working dogs have an extremely high desire for the toy or the reward," said Serella. "We only play with that reward when they are working and after they have done a good job and have met the standard. That's their form of currency."

For the first two or three months after a dog reports for duty, both handler and base trainers work to bring a dog up to the highest level possible through a certification process where every bit of work done by dog and human, alone and together, is analyzed and critiqued. "The bond with the handler is imperative," said Tech. Sgt. Kenneth Clinton, kennel master with the 31st Security Forces Squadron at Aviano Air Base in Italy. "The initial phase of the certification process is having the handler build rapport with the dog. Without trust and respect, the dog team is fighting each other, the dog isn't going to want to do anything for the handler and the handler won't trust the dog's instincts."

"Building rapport is more like having to make someone your best friend,"

said S.Sgt. Erick Parris, a handler who works alongside Clinton in the 31st SFS. "It has to be sincere, if you don't truly love your dog they can tell. It's easy for me though, I genuinely love my pup."

"My job is to make sure the dogs go through the hardest training they can go through," said Tech. Sgt. Manuel Gamboa, a trainer with the 31st SFS who certifies new recruits at the base. "That way, when they do become qualified, they are ready for anything."

With Greco working alongside Serella, it was clear that the dog was well on his way.

2

ACTIVE DUTY

Once an MWD is certified he's ready to serve on active duty, whether at a military base in the United States or deployed overseas. As a rule, each dog is matched with a base and stays with the base until he retires, while handlers tend to be switched to a different canine partner every two years, though it's not unheard of for a handler and MWD to be a team for longer than that; indeed, countless handlers have decided to reenlist simply because their canine partner had another year or two to go before he could retire.

Civilians rarely have an idea of the bond that dog and handler form and share over the course of working together for two—or more—years, especially if they're deployed overseas. If the team serves by providing patrol and detection services at a military base, it's standard for handlers to go home at the end of the day while canines head to their kennels; however, when deployed, MWD teams can easily spend every waking hour together.

S.Sgt. Alexandra Springman, a handler with the 355th Security Forces Squadron at Davis-Monthan Air Force Base in Arizona, was teamed up with a German shepherd named Dexter who was certified as both a patrol and explosive-detection dog. While Springman obviously appreciated her multi-talented partner, she particularly appreciated him once they deployed.

"Deploying helped Dexter and myself grow and bond because it was just the two of us," she said. "He solely looked to me for everything. I was always the one who fed him every morning and every evening, took him to go to the bathroom, groomed him and bathed him. Also, when we were deployed, he lived in my room with me, so we literally spent 24 hours a day together."

Tech. Sgt. Chad Eagan, a handler based at Cannon Air Force Base in New Mexico agreed. "The most enjoyable part is being able to deploy with your best friend," he said.

NAVY: BRIT

All deployments can be stressful, especially when they're your first. So when PO 3rd Class Daniel Padilla received orders for his first overseas mission, his stress was slightly alleviated when he learned he'd be teamed up with PO 2nd Class Brit, an explosive-detection dog who already had a few deployments under his belt, uh, *collar*.

"[Brit] is a very experienced dog and has been deployed a few times with other handlers, so when we get out there I am sure he will show me a few things," Padilla said.

After receiving their orders to head to Djibouti, Padilla and Brit trained for more than six months. "We spend every day together," Padilla said. "We train constantly, playing detection games. We also do obedience training where we practice different commands and throw a ball around.

"Everything we both learned will be put to the test," he added. While he admitted to being nervous as well as a little excited, the fact that he and Brit were heading there together made a huge difference. "It's different because I am not going alone; I am going with my buddy so I will have someone to play and work with."

AIR FORCE: CIRO

Whether a canine team is deployed in a war zone or serving stateside examining visitors and active military on a base for contraband or patrol, handlers have additional responsibilities that non-handlers don't have:

In addition to taking care of themselves, they must also care for their four-legged partners regardless of how harsh the environment. "We do the same details [as other security forces airmen], but we have the additional responsibility of having to care for and train these animals," said Senior Airman Carrie

Dowdy, based at Tyndall Air Force Base in Florida, where she is paired with a German shepherd named Ciro.

That applies to providing food and water and making sure he gets enough rest but also carrying extra equipment for the dog, which is particularly impor-

tant when working in desert zones. From booties that protect a dog's sensitive paws from 120-degree asphalt to Doggles that shield their eyes from searing sun and sandstorms, a handler must always be prepared whether the team is training several hours a day or conducting active patrol beyond the wire. In addition to carrying canine-sized equipment, handlers must also tote a first-aid kit and know how to treat their dogs in case of a medical emergency. In a desert environment, this includes administering IV fluids in case their canine partners suffer heatstroke or dehydration.

"They're just like us," Dowdy said, adding that she is constantly humbled by the job she and Ciro perform. "Ciro and I are learning something new every day together."

ARMY: ANDY, ALEX, NIKO, AND LEE: A TEAM EFFORT

Though many MWD teams serve as the sole canine duo in a particular unit, on tougher assignments it sometimes takes a village of multiple MWD teams in order to get the job done. At Bagram Airfield in Afghanistan in the summer of 2015, a group of four handler teams worked together to support a mission from the 101st Airborne Division out of Fort Campbell, Kentucky. The team's job—singularly and collectively—was to find IEDs, short for "Improvised Explosive Devices." Once a dog alerts to the scent of an explosive, an explosive-ordnance disposal team is summoned since disarming an IED is not part of an MWD team's job description.

"Out here [we do] a lot of route clearance," said Spc. Craig Holbrook, who works with his canine partner, Niko, alongside three other MWD teams: Spc. Anthony Andrews and Andy, Spc. Ethan Taylor and Alex, and Spc. Joseph Mora and Lee. "It's an entire dog team effort, not just the dog or the handler," he added.

After spending the majority of their waking hours together, first training to prepare for deployment and then after they've arrived at their overseas posting, most handlers immediately know when their canine partner has detected

a scent. "After you've been with a dog long enough you know exactly how he acts," said Holbrook. "A lot of us are able to tell when our dog smells an explosive by even the most subtle changes in our dog's behavior. Sometimes it's something so subtle that other people can't even tell that he is acting any dif-

ferently, but we've trained with them so much that we can pick it up."

After the nerves and stress of being outside the wire, one part of the job that both members of the team look forward to is the reward: the toy or ball. "This is a game for the dog and we make it as fun as we can for them," Taylor said.

Though dog and handler are joined at the hip while stateside, handlers frequently say that it's only when both are deployed that the true skill and character of their dogs shows through. "Having a military working dog as a partner is an amazing experience that you can only fully understand by deploying as a

Microsoft Excel

CAUTION MILITARY
WORKING DOG

ب عقب استاده شو
سانه کار سگهای
قرار دادی

35

ATLANTIC CITY

military working dog team," Andrews said. "Andy is an amazing dog and he is really great at what he does. Andy is more than just a dog, he's my best friend and will always have a special place in my heart. I would do anything for Andy and I know he would do the same for me."

COAST GUARD: NUCKY AND RICKY

The Coast Guard has a long history of employing mascots around the base, not necessarily as patrol or detection dogs but because, more often than not, a stray dog shows up and endears himself to the crew. Before you know it, the canine has a rank, a place to sleep, and a whole slew of responsibilities. It's safe to say that one requirement is that the dog should love the water, though there have been exceptions here and there.

The Coast Guard base in Atlantic City, New Jersey, is home to a New-foundland named Nucky, short for "Nucklas," who has proven to be so adept at his job—which includes catching mooring lines in his mouth, greeting visitors, and drooling prodigiously, as Newfies are known to do—that he was promoted from seaman apprentice to petty officer third class only a couple of years after showing up on the job. "He is disappointed every time the boat leaves," said PO 1st Class Christopher Fonseca, who is in charge of training at the station. "He is on the pier barking and cheering when we return, which is a boost of morale after a long day patrolling the waters."

During training exercises, crew members are expected to get certifications and maintain them based on Coast Guard crew proficiency standards. These exercises are challenging, and all crew members are required to maintain proficiency, including Nucky. "When we jump into the water, he jumps in with us," said Seaman Madison Wood, a crew member at the station. "It makes the training more enjoyable for everyone when he's around." After all, Nucky is a water dog and likes to go swimming on a regular basis. "He doesn't ask for permission or authorization for swim calls," said Fonseca. Nucky also runs with boat crew members during their bi-annual physical fitness test and tends to finish in the same amount of time it takes eighteen to twenty-nine-year-olds.

In recent years, like other branches in the military, Coast Guard bases have brought more specialized MWD teams into their ranks as well. Over on the other side of the country, the Coast Guard Station San Francisco has stepped up its activity to protect San Francisco Bay, which isn't a surprise: 1,445 container ships docked at the port of Oakland in 2014, making it the fifth-busiest seaport in the United States.

For this reason, the Coast Guard base specifically works with specially trained bomb-sniffing dogs. "We want to have the ability to handle any kind of threat we encounter offshore and away from the port environment," said Coast Guard ME1 Chris Hartman, a handler at the base.

MWD teams have to be prepared to hoist themselves out of helicopters and land on the deck of a boat or ship, so PO 1st Class Ricky, a Belgian Malinois who trains alongside his handler, PO Jordan Brosowski, conducts regular

training sessions where they practice everything from flying in a helicopter to being hoisted in and out of it. Indeed, humans also appreciate the extra training.

"It makes it that much more difficult to complete a hoist when you have a 60-pound dog that's freaking out," said Brosowski, since even the most highly trained MWDs can panic due to the noise, wind, and instability of a chopper.

"Some dogs are very aggressive and they might try to bite my leg," said hoist operator Ben Schmidt, who is clearly in a position to bear the brunt of the fury if a dog decides he doesn't want to be seventy-five feet in the air after all. "You can see on the hoist the dog's mouth is about an inch from my leg."

But Ricky and his two canine teammates passed the test with flying colors, helped in no small part by Brosowski's constant reassurances. "I kept petting his back and his neck, telling him he was a good boy and letting him know everything was going to be OK," Brosowski said.

MARINES: WILLY PETE

Not all dogs on active duty come up through the ranks the usual way. Some are strays who simply appear one day, and the troops adopt them to provide a

little bit of softness in what can be an extremely harsh environment. However, sometimes to show his gratitude the canine will spring into action, proving to be a true soldier.

That's just what happened at a Marine base in Helmand Province in Afghanistan in 2009 when the Marines of Company D adopted a couple of stray dogs—one of them pregnant—and named them Sandy and Scraggles. When Sandy gave birth, the Marines decided to keep one of the puppies and name him Willy Pete. The young pup was a quick learner, tagging along with the

Marines on base and patrolling alongside them to protect the base. Soon the Marines started to take him on missions outside the wire.

One day a squad of Marines—including Willy Pete—was patrolling in a nearby village known as Dog Town, named after the community of wild dogs that were living there. "All of the dogs were overly aggressive and tried to stop the patrol's movement by intimidating the Marines," said Sgt. Joshua Davis. "Willy Pete singlehandedly fought off five wild dogs to protect them. After Willy engaged the dogs, my squad was able to push through the village to complete our patrol."

"He is a proven veteran and a wounded warrior," said S.Sgt. Anthony J. Eichler. "Willy is always tirelessly watching over what I would assume he considers 'his' Marines. He is a friend of all Marines, and he works hard every day on patrol and for [our] security. He's been knocked down a few times, but continues on with the mission just like any Marine would be expected to do."

"Willy never walks in the other direction or tries to hide when he sees a squad heading out for a patrol," added Lance Cpl. Philip Bulford. "I believe that Willy believes it's his duty and an honor to protect us from what may lie ahead."

★★★ (3) ★★★

CONTINUING EDUCATION

The training for an MWD never ends.

Ever.

Even at night and in all kinds of weather and environments: in water, the pitch black of night, jumping out of helicopters.

"Just like Marines, if we don't continue the dogs' training, it can easily diminish and they will forget things," said Cpl. Sean McKenzie, a handler based at the Marine Corps base in Okinawa, Japan. "It's important to keep on training because in the event that a team is needed immediately, the dogs can do what they are tasked to do."

"We're constantly training, constantly improving," said Tech. Sgt. Chad Eagan, a handler based at Cannon Air Force Base in New Mexico. "Detection is the main reason our dogs are here, so that's what we focus on."

Training never stops for the dogs, even when they are deployed; in fact, if anything, it ratchets up whenever an MWD team is sent to a new area with unknown and strange smells, people, and terrain. It also serves to strengthen an already tight bond between dog and human.

"Deployments are probably one of the most bonding experiences an MWD team can have," said S.Sgt. Jessie Johnson, a handler with the 56th Security Forces Squadron at Luke Air Force Base in Arizona. "There wasn't more than two hours a day when I wasn't with my dog. I needed him to protect myself and the team, and he needed me to take care of his daily needs."

"You get attached to different units, so a lot of the time your dog is your only friend," said S.Sgt. Daniel Andrzejewski, kennel master at Marine Corps Base Camp Butler in Okinawa, Japan. "You eat together. You sleep together. You play together. Wherever you go, the dog goes."

When deployed, MWD teams frequently have to improvise, assembling rudimentary obstacle courses from whatever materials they can find, but once they're back at their home base they train at a dedicated well-equipped facility. However, if the chance comes to train in a real-world building or environment like a football stadium or a school, handlers and trainers usually grab it.

"We pretty much stay on the installations, but now we are starting to build up a better point-of-contact training schedule so that we can leave installations and come out to areas like this," said Sgt. 1st Class Raymond Richardson, kennel master at Joint Base Myer–Henderson Hall in Landover, Maryland, referring to a recent MWD training exercise at FedExField. "The stadium itself is insanely large, and challenges the handlers as well, not only the dogs. [Commercial] kitchens are also great, because they smell like food and grease, which are good distractions for the dogs."

"The training should be a fun experience for the dogs," said S.Sgt. Charles Hardesty, kennel master at the Marine Corps Air Ground Combat Center in Twentynine Palms, California. "If the dog thinks training is going to get him in trouble, it is not going to do its job."

The constant training and ongoing vigilance don't just benefit the dogs, but the handlers as well. "The dogs teach you something every day," said Air Force S.Sgt. Jessie Johnson, a handler based at Luke Air Force Base in Arizona. "There is never a time you can say you've taught a dog everything or that a handler knows everything. I learn every day. I've never been so happy to want to go to work."

WATER TRAINING: EVERYBODY IN THE POOL!

Just as many two-legged soldiers may be called to respond quickly in any possible kind of environment—from blazing-hot deserts to a subzero Arctic blizzard—the same goes for canine soldiers. Even though water training is not a standard part of most MWD training regimens, many bases do occasionally

provide the opportunity to their MWD teams.

"[Most] dogs have been trained for a desert environment," said Cpl. Jonathan Scudder, a handler at the Marine Corps Air Ground Combat Center in Twentynine Palms, California. "Exposing them to water prepares them for

46

where they may go when they change stations or handlers."

He added that while some dogs take to the training like, well, a duck to water, some are more reluctant. "How quickly a dog gets accustomed to training in and around water depends on each individual dog and the handler's training," Scudder noted. "We take baby steps to ease them into the idea of swimming and practicing what they know while in water. It's best described as success of approximation."

Cpl. Paul Kelley, a handler also based at Twentynine Palms, believes it's imperative that every canine soldier acquire some practice doing his job in a water environment. "If a working dog gets deployed with a handler to a combat zone and the Marine has to swim a distance with his rifle and combat load, he has to have confidence that his dog will be able to follow him effectively," Kelley said. "We have to prepare them for where they may go. As handlers we have to make sure we keep training to build that confidence with them."

FLYING

Just as there are many people who are not crazy about flying, the same applies to dogs, including those who serve in the military.

But because canine soldiers are so often called upon to travel to far corners

of the world, it's a necessary evil. However, there's a big difference between traveling in a cargo plane and jumping out of a helicopter and / or shimmying down a rope while a chopper hovers noisily overhead. That's why many military bases have ramped up training in recent years.

Handler Sgt. Nina Alero, for one, would have welcomed the training since she and Rex, her canine partner, already had to board a helicopter with no previous training. "Rex was stressed out because of all the noise, it was like sensory overload for him," Alero said. "This training would have been beneficial to have prior, so I could have known my dog's reaction to getting in and out of the chopper."

Previous training would have benefited those military personnel who rescue others as well. "Most pararescuemen have never hoisted dogs into a helicopter before, so this [training session] was an experiment to see how the dogs would react to the sound of the helicopters and being in air," said S.Sgt. Kenneth O'Brien, a pararescueman with the 83rd Expeditionary Rescue Squadron based at Bagram Airfield in Afghanistan.

One way to meet the need for such high-wire training is to practice by rappelling, which is referred to in the military as fast-roping. Camp Hansen in Okinawa, Japan, has a dedicated rope tower where Marines can practice with and without their dogs.

"The [fast-roping] . . . was a lot

different because you had a dog on your back, and he is moving around," said Lance Cpl. David Hernandez, a handler with the 3rd Marine Expeditionary Force at the camp. "This is an experience most dog handlers do not get to have."

Cpl. Nicholas Mejerus, another handler at Camp Hansen, agrees. "If we were to get attached to a unit that is trying to do an air assault, and that handler dog team had never done that kind of training before, they wouldn't know what to do," he said, adding that with the experience under their belt, they can help guide others, through either a simulated exercise or the real thing. "Now that we have done it, we can share our knowledge with other Marines."

NIGHT VISION

War is a 24/7 business. That's why canine soldiers and their handlers often train under cover of darkness so they're prepared for anything.

At the Marine Corps Air Ground Combat Center in Twentynine Palms,

California, canine soldiers and their handlers conduct night-training exercises at least once every month. "At night is when the dogs would usually work," said S.Sgt. Daniel Andrzejewski, former kennel master at the base. "So on top of any other training the handlers do, we also do this night training."

While many handlers would prefer to work with their canine partners in the light of day, others clearly prefer the nighttime hours. "We're down and out of the way," said S.Sgt. Michael Caruso, an MWD handler who works alongside his partner, Zody, at the 51st Security Forces Squadron at the Osan Air Base in South Korea. "We'll be able to see someone and before they know what's going on, I can notify base security operations to dispatch responders to handle the potential threat."

Typically, such training is conducted at venues that are not part of the dogs' regular routines in an effort to challenge their senses and allow them to

practice in unfamiliar places.

"We plant the [training scents] . . . in different locations throughout the building and let them sit there for about thirty minutes," Andrzejewski said. "After that, the scent has had time to spread around the room and give the dog a better chance to find it. Most of the time, the substance will be sitting in a hiding spot for a longer period of time."

CHOMP!

Perhaps the most commonly used photo in stories about military working dogs is one that shows them in action, that is, biting the arm of a pretend bad guy. Certainly, showing a picture of a snarling, growling, tooth-baring canine can be an effective way to demonstrate the essence of what a military working dog is capable of and why the military values them so much, but the truth is that it's rare for a canine soldier to get a chance to bite an actual villain outside of training.

In short, MWDs are trained to bite because it builds and displays aggression in a dog, which is a required personality trait for all canine soldiers. Though similar to the firearms practice and training that law enforcement professionals endure, it may never be necessary to fire a gun in the line of duty.

"Aggression and biting are skills we need the dogs to have even if we aren't going to use it," said S.Sgt. Charles Hardesty. "It's all about building confidence. If the handlers are timid, the dogs are going to sense that and act the same way. We have to build their confidence and then reinforce it with positive feedback."

"We like to take it step by step with aggression," said S.Sgt. Daniel Andrzejewski. "Training varies from dog to dog. We work them up with different biting wraps because we don't want the dogs to become gear dependent."

Whether a handler opts to use a bite sleeve or a full-body bite suit that

tends to make the pretend "bad guy" look like the Michelin Man, depends on the trainer and handler as well as the specific exercise, but the actual bite is only the beginning of the training. S.Sgt. Conan Thomas and his canine partner, Sgt. 1st Class Britt, continued their training while deployed to Iraq from Fort Carson, Colorado. "Britt is trained on a bite sleeve, but we like to use a whole bite suit just for the safety of the decoy," said Thomas. "How a [human] decoy acts when he goes down is important to make the training good for the dog. The drive for the dog is the bite, and he can't bite without us having at least a bite sleeve."

As is the case with other facets of MWD training, the handler learns just as much as the canine, sometimes even more. "Getting bit by your dog allows you to understand what the suspect is going through, just like when we use Tasers and pepper spray on one another in training," said S.Sgt. Gary Cheney, a handler with the 633rd Security Forces Squadron at Langley Air Force Base in Virginia. "The tactical bite suit made it more realistic. The dog recognizes the suspect is in pain and knows what to do."

MAY THE BEST DOG WIN

In addition to the certifications and tests that every canine soldier has to pass on a regular basis, many also participate in regular competitions and races that pit them against other MWD teams—and sometimes civilians—so their handlers can better determine just how fit they are and how well they work together.

Some of these contests are produced by outside sporting groups and non-profit veterans' organizations, but a handful are run by the Department of Defense. These Military Working Dog Trials offer MWD teams from military bases from across the country the opportunity to compete in a series of events that test their mettle in both speed and form. To be sure, these contests can be quite grueling, but it was the Iron Dog competition, a demanding six-mile obstacle course where handlers are outfitted in full combat gear while wearing a rucksack that contained a thirty-five-pound sandbag, that served as the true challenge for both human and dog. Once they're geared up, participants were required

to run through often rough terrain—occasionally hoisting their canine partners onto their backs—rescue a lifeless body from a vulnerable area, and crawl under barbed-wire fences while simulated gunfire screamed inches above their heads.

"[The competition] allowed us to handle scenarios we may actually come across here or while deployed," said PO 1st Class Ekali Brooks, an MWD trainer with the 341st Training Squadron at Joint Base San Antonio–Lackland.

Brooks—who won in two categories and was awarded the overall title of "Top Dog" following the three-day Military Working Dog Trial at Lackland in 2012—added that despite every competitor's desire to win, or at least finish, the Trials and Iron Dog course also served as a valuable training aid for each and every handler. "We were able to help each other by pointing out the good or bad things we saw. In the end, it makes us all better handlers," he said.

Marine S.Sgt. Jessy Eslick, who works with the Defense Department's Research and Development Section, said that watching the competitors—both human and canine—made him realize that despite standard MWD training practices every MWD team is required to meet, a great deal of diversity in training techniques and maneuvers is employed by trainers and handlers at bases across the country and on deployments.

"The dog world is changing every day and we need to stay on top of the new technology and training techniques," said Eslick. "That being said, we have some

work to do to improve and learn from the handlers and trainers before us. I have pride in being part of such a special group of individuals who are dedicated to improving every day. When the time comes and you're asked to go out on the front lines, you know that you and your dog are there to save lives. You can't ask for a greater responsibility than being a dog handler."

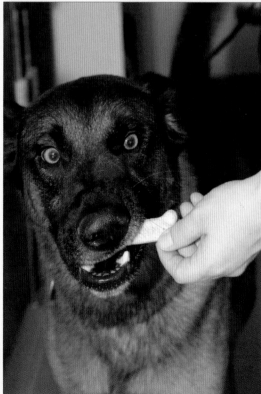

★★★ (4) ★★★
MOONLIGHTING

MWDs are so well trained that it's no surprise that they are in great demand not only by other governmental departments but also by local law enforcement agencies.

For example, many MWDs and their handlers are called upon every four years to work alongside local police departments and other government agencies to conduct security sweeps and keep an eye out during the Republican and Democratic National Conventions. In other cases, special sporting events—such as the World Series—mean that highly trained canine soldiers are the easiest and fastest way to clear a scene as well as screen visitors at the door.

But sometimes the request is more informal. Indeed, sometimes they're even asked to moonlight by other service members on base who just need to plunge their hands into a dog's fur for an instant pick-me-up.

Whatever the case, it's good to know that at least in most instances moonlighting isn't frowned upon by the boss.

LOCAL LAW ENFORCEMENT

Military dog teams are often called upon by municipal and county police and sheriff departments in their areas simply because they can respond more

quickly to an emergency; this could be because they're physically closer to an incident or the resident canine police team is out on another call or serving on a patrol miles away.

When a bomb threat was called into the Rodney E. Thompson Middle School in Stafford, Virginia, the first point of contact was the Stafford County Sheriff's Office, but the dispatcher wanted an MWD team from the Marine Corps Base in Quantico to respond to the call as well. "We had one of our dogs on scene, but for an incident like this, we wanted to be able to check the scene as fast as we can," said Bill Kennedy, public information officer with the sheriff's department.

Handler Lance Cpl. Alton Davis and his canine partner, Jesse, arrived on the scene and immediately got to work, divvying up the search territory with the canine team from the sheriff's office. As a result, they were able to scope out and clear the entire school in half the time it would normally take. "If we can get somewhere in a timely manner to eliminate the threat, then that's what needs to be done for the best of the community," said Davis.

The school search wasn't the first cooperative effort between MWD teams at Quantico and the sheriff's department. "We get calls like these every few months," said Davis. "There are only so many explosive canine units about in town and when they can't respond, we are called to support them. It's easy to work together and get the job done."

Kennedy concurs that it certainly makes his job—and that of his colleagues—easier. "The handlers and their dogs are always professional," he said.

"Working together is a huge benefit, especially [when they respond in] such a timely manner."

SPECIAL EVENTS

The frequency of how often MWD teams are called upon to moonlight is often dictated by their location. As a matter of course, MWD teams who serve at the Coast Guard base in San Francisco are kept pretty busy with their own responsibilities in addition to pitching in to help local police departments and nearby federal agencies keep the entire Bay Area safe. After all, the region is a rich coastal area with hundreds of events every year that take place on or near the water and can potentially attract tens of thousands of people to each one. As a result, MWD teams often help to patrol and provide crowd control while also conducting regular sweeps of the piers, ferries, downtown area, and even AT&T Park before baseball games.

In late 2015, they performed helicopter training in the area to prepare for Super Bowl 50, held at Levi's Stadium in Santa Clara, California, in February 2016. "In the event of an emergency during Super Bowl 50, there will be a significant impact on ground transportation," said Lt. Neil Penso, a pilot serving at Air Station San Francisco. "Transporting canines and their handlers from site to site may require a helicopter." And even though the Coast Guard canines regularly practice helicopter maneuvers, they scheduled the special training to help teach dogs working at other federal, state, and local law enforcement departments, while it served as a refresher course for themselves.

"The exercise is outside normal duties for partner agencies," said Coast Guard ME1 Chris Hartman. "Our canines are accustomed to the noise of the engines and familiar with the cabin of the helicopters, while other agencies may not be. In an event of an emergency, the other departments need to know what to expect in case they have to deploy aboard one to get to a location."

Neil Wu, with the U.S. Park Police force, appreciated the training. "It's better to find out how the dogs handle it now than later."

PROTECTING VIPS

Some MWD teams moonlight so frequently that it's almost like they're holding down two jobs at the same time. These hardworking canines toil endlessly at their home bases, sniffing for bad guys and / or explosives, but whenever a foreign dignitary—like the Pope or the leader of a foreign country—comes to town or the President of the United States decides to go on a jaunt to a local bookstore in Washington, D.C., the canine teams spring into action.

This is the case more often than not for the twenty-seven MWD teams who work for the 947th Military Police Detachment, which is located at both Joint Base Myer–Henderson Hall in Arlington, Virginia and Fort Belvoir in Fairfax County, Virginia. Whether it's the Secret Service or a local police department in charge of making sure an area is secure for a visiting VIP, the majority of MWD teams are on call 24 / 7 at any given time and must be ready

to report for duty at a moment's notice. After all, as Army Lt. Col. Macedonio Molina, director of Emergency Services at Joint Base Myer–Henderson Hall, put it, "If bad guys know the dogs are working, they are less likely to do something."

"Our [operations] tempo is like none other I've ever seen in the twelve years since I've been doing this, from the President all the way down to all the foreign dignitaries and most recently the Pope mission," said Sgt. 1st Class Raymond Richardson, kennel master for the 947th.

"Anytime the President goes somewhere, we have to go with him," said Sgt. Charles Ogin, a handler for the team. "We're working the road, doing missions, and possibly deploying for nine to twelve months; it's just always hectic."

Fellow handler Sgt. Wes Brown concurs. "As a dog handler you're going everywhere," he said. "I was in Berlin, Turkey, Russia, Afghanistan, so on and

so forth." Regardless of the schedule and the challenges and unpredictability, team members say they wouldn't have it any other way because of the invaluable service they bring to others.

"There's no way to put a price tag on how important this job actually is," said Richardson.

EMOTIONAL RESCUE

While it's no secret that the presence of a highly trained MWD can work wonders in serving as a welcome distraction for passersby—even if the canine soldier is in working mode and wearing his DO NOT PET collar—when he is off the clock and people are welcome to pet him blood pressure drops and there are smiles all around.

This is the primary impetus behind a unique program where some canine soldiers are moonlighting at a job where they're actively helping speed the re-

covery and rehabilitation of soldiers who have been injured in the line of duty or have an illness that requires them to rest.

At Joint Base Balad in Iraq, several MWD teams regularly visit patients at the Air Force Theater Hospital. "We're working together to make patients  feel good about themselves and about healing," said S.Sgt. Janice Shipman, a medical technician with the 332nd Expeditionary Medical Group who launched the project. "From my experience, patients focus on their injuries so much that just being able to have a distraction even for a little bit helps them heal. It's very therapeutic."

Interacting with patients and medical staff also helps the dogs with their training. "These are military working dogs, so when they are on duty on base we generally do not let people pet them," said Tech. Sgt. Joseph Throgmorton, kennel master at the base. "However, we have a unique mission here. Our dogs are working with non-canine handlers in close quarters of vehicles off-base and need to become comfortable around others."

S.Sgt. Kristen Smith, a canine handler, has witnessed firsthand just how valuable this extracurricular activity has been while training and working with her canine partner, Cezar. "Whenever you're training the dog around Coalition forces, you want to make sure he's not aggressing on people you don't want him to aggress on," she explained. "This program furthers that training because when we are riding in Humvees and are out patrolling, we try to train the dogs on how to act around Coalition forces so that they're only going to act aggressively whenever they feel threatened, his handler is threatened or when given the actual command."

It's clear that patients welcome the program. While he was a patient at the hospital, Army S.Sgt. Vannell Baerrien realized that spending time with the dogs definitely helped him recover quickly. "Being here with the dogs has helped me relax a lot more," he said. "It has helped me to be able to take a deep breath and exhale."

Sergeant Shipman noticed an unexpected, additional benefit: as the dogs spent more time on the medical floor interacting with patients, hospital staff learned about the MWD program and the MWD teams became educated about the therapies and programs offered at the hospital, therefore providing a big push towards bringing people at the base together and showing that they share a common purpose. "The canine unit sees what we do as a medical staff, and the medical staff sees what the MWDs can do. They save lives just like we do. We work together with the common goal to heal our patients."

(5)

PUBLIC AFFAIRS

Though MWD handlers speak a language all their own when it comes to communicating with their canine partners—often without opening their mouths—they must frequently interact with people who have no idea what life is like with an MWD or, indeed, what to expect from a simple encounter. "Can I pet the doggie?" most ask, or maybe they're afraid of all dogs, especially ones that can look so ferocious.

That's where the role of public affairs comes in, where handler and canine set out to educate both civilians and fellow military personnel and staff on exactly what these dogs are capable of, from charging a bad guy in a bite suit to rolling onto their backs for a few well-earned belly rubs.

"Letting people know what we do and that we're here to help them, helps us," said Cpl. Darren Westmoreland, a handler at the Marine Corps Air Ground Combat Center in Twentynine Palms, California. Plus, having the dogs interact with—and occasionally show off for—civilians only enhances their training. "Putting the dogs into a scenario with a crowd helps them train

[because they] . . . still have to perform their tasks regardless of people's reactions," he added.

Public affairs demonstrations can include everything from participating in a library program designed to help children improve their reading to running the dogs through their daily training regimen at a demonstration on the grounds of a local county or state fair. Public affairs also extend to deployment, when human and canine soldiers in a war zone can help ease the stress and strain of the situation by showing local civilians that these dogs, while professionally trained as soldiers, are not something to fear.

"We're here to show them some of the capabilities our teams bring to the troops in the field," said S.Sgt. Jeffery Worley, kennel master at the Marine Corps air station in Yuma, Arizona. "We're out here showing them what we can do, what we love to do. It's always a privilege to show what our dogs are capable of, and help people better understand what it is we do."

READING

Sometimes reluctant readers need a nudge of encouragement to help them pursue what they often find to be a difficult task, whether it's reading an entire book by themselves cover to cover for the first time or tackling a higher reading level. If that nudge comes in the form of a wet nose, furry body, and marvelous jumps and leaps through the air, so much the better; more kids just might be persuaded to pick up a book and soldier on through.

At the Marine Corps Air Ground Combat Center in Twentynine Palms, California, a German shepherd named Colli served as a welcome and inspirational reward for the kids participating in Paws for Reading, a summertime reading program at the base library, where librarians joined with the MWD

teams on base to provide a draw for kids in the form of a working-dog demonstration.

And what an incentive. As the kids crouched on the edge of a field, several handlers ran their dogs through their standard obedience routines and the onlookers gasped, laughed, and applauded. But once the bite suit came out, the kids sat up straighter and were clearly riveted. A handler in the bulky suit started to run while another handler held Colli and riled him up before releasing him. In a matter of seconds the dog was hanging off one arm growling and snarling while the "perpetrator" wore a huge smile . . . along with the children.

"I love using our on-base resources to provide different events for kids," said Ursula Morales, program coordinator at the base library. "The program helps younger children stay engaged in reading over the summer to avoid what's called 'summer slide' where students will regress in their reading if they don't keep their minds active. To avoid that we include incentives to keep participants interested."

COMMUNITY DEMONSTRATIONS

While there's a fair chance that kids who live with their parents on a military base have already seen canine soldiers just by virtue of living there, the same can't be said for civilians in the local community.

So it makes sense to introduce the public to the talents and skills of canine soldiers at an event where people normally come to see and visit with other animals as a matter of course. For many people in Washington State, that event would be the annual Puyallup Fair at summer's end. Traditionally, in addition to the livestock exhibits and ox pulls, the fair also showcases other animals, including dogs from rescue groups and guide dog organizations, so a group of MWDs from the nearby 51st Military Police Detachment at Joint Base Lewis-

McChord fit right in.

"The goal was to put a face with the military canine program and working dog teams here," said handler Sgt. Todd Neveu, who works alongside S.Sgt. Gizmo, a German shepherd. "Puyallup wants to showcase the local dog handlers and we are a part of that, showing what our dogs can do."

Hands-on demonstrations that provide local residents with a chance to pet the dogs, interact with them up close, and ask questions of their handlers also help to defuse any natural tension that civilians might feel when they see a police car carrying a dog out in the community, whether it belongs to the military or local police force. Across the country from the Puyallup Fair at the Army base in Fort Campbell, Kentucky, handlers and their canine partners often visit local schools and community organizations to give talks about the MWD program. S.Sgt. Jonathan Rose runs the MWD program at the base

and says it's a good chance to build bonds between military and locals.

"It shows them that we're here and we're available, and it teaches them about the capabilities we have," said Rose. "A lot of people don't know who we work for or what we do. They think we just drive around in patrol cars eating doughnuts and drinking coffee. I'm just showing them the other side of the house. Besides, this is a job in the military that they might not know that is available to them."

FUTURE HANDLERS

Although securing a position as part of a MWD team in any branch of the military is highly competitive among humans as well as canines, the various branches never stop recruiting for new members; after all, it's the only way to find the absolute cream of the crop. As a result, many MWD units hold regular demonstrations for prospective soldiers, often for members of the Reserve Officers' Training Corps, who are based on college campuses, as well as its junior division program at high schools across the country.

This form of community service can also cross borders. When a group from the Canadian Air Cadet Program, a youth program similar to JROTC, visited Joint Base Langley-Eustis in Virginia, they got a behind-the-scenes

peek at operations on the base, but they especially perked up when the MWD demonstration began.

"It's important to share our American military culture with our international allies so they can get a better understanding of the way we operate," said

Tech. Sgt. Mark Leslie, the kennel master at the base who led the demonstration. "While conducting joint operations, many service members have the opportunity to work hand-in-hand with other nations, and sharing our culture and understanding each other is a necessity to working together."

One of the Canadian cadets, Rolan Naiman, a warrant officer with the 180th Mosquito Squadron, thought the MWD demonstration was a perfect way to showcase the breadth and diversity of the U.S. military. "Within our cadet program, we can be in our own 'bubble' in Canada," he admitted. Since the Canadian Air Cadet Program actively encourages the idea of building connections with military personnel and civilians throughout the world, providing their service members with experience and demonstrations give cadets first-hand experience and may just spark an interest in becoming a MWD handler on their own.

The handlers who give the demonstrations also benefit. "Personally, I like having fun with the kids while also trying to teach them something about the mission," said Leslie.

HEARTS AND MINDS

It's all well and good when demonstrations that spotlight the amazing things that MWD can do are essentially preaching to the choir. But it turns into a much different—and potentially tense—job when a handler uses her canine partner to reach out to a person who may have been afraid of dogs his entire life. Even more difficult is bridging the cultural gap with people who grew up in a society that teaches that dogs are unclean and have no place interacting with humans, much less living in the same house with them. Indeed, in some Arab cultures people believe that if a dog eats from a plate that humans eat from, the plate must be scoured with sand and placed in a sunny spot for forty days in order to purify it.

So MWD teams who serve in Muslim countries in the Middle East, such as Iraq and Afghanistan, must overcome a centuries (indeed, millennia) old distrust of dogs. Add to this the fact that many residents of Iraq and Afghanistan view the military as invaders and occupiers and the presence of a dog adds insult to injury in their eyes. For handlers and their dogs on deployment, this is obviously a trickier situation than setting up a couple of high hurdles and donning bite suits in order to display their talents and win the crowd.

One way that U.S. Coalition handlers have worked to bridge the gap in recent wars and conflicts is to help the Iraqi and Afghani police form their own MWD program and train in clear view of locals, helping them to realize that if one of their

own could work with a dog to help fight terrorism in their own backyards then maybe dogs aren't such a bad thing after all.

In the spring of 2010, Coalition forces paired up with a team of five Iraqi police officers with five dogs and, after just six weeks of training, the teams were already succeeding in finding reserves of explosives and bombs hidden in neighborhood houses. As curious residents gathered to watch Mahmoud Ismail Husain, one of the first group of five, search local buildings with his canine partner Bally, a Belgian Malinois, Husain soon found himself teaching his neighbors what his dog could do, things he had just learned himself a few weeks earlier.

"I encourage them not to fear the dog," said Husain. "I tell people that Bally is a working dog and he is here to protect our country. He doesn't bite—he finds explosives."

And just like his more experienced MWD handlers, Husain never stops being amused and entertained by his canine partner. "When I laid eyes on him, I knew he was going to be my dog just from his stance, he was very athletic and hyper," he said. "Bally is a troublemaker. When he gets hold of his toy, he doesn't let go. He makes me very tired."

But it's not only the police and military who are helping people in Arab countries learn that dogs are not to be feared. Operation Outreach Afghanistan, an organization that provides humanitarian support and equipment as well as food and clothing to Afghanis throughout the country, is also spreading the word about MWDs.

The group regularly schedules Kids Day for local children, including pizza for lunch, English lessons, and demonstrations by Coalition canine teams and military veterinary staffers. While they didn't bring out the bite suit, they did show the kids how to care for a dog, from feeding to grooming, and even held an informal dog show that featured the MWDs. For some kids, the highlight

of the day was when they donned a stethoscope and listened to a dog's heartbeat for the first time.

PREACHING TO THE CHOIR

Though it's clear that the vast majority of nonmilitary who view a canine demonstration thoroughly enjoy seeing the dogs strut their stuff, perhaps the audience that appreciates them the most consists of other military veterans.

For the MWD teams from Camp Lejeune in Jacksonville, North Carolina, one of their favorite ways to give back is with demonstrations for groups

of local veterans from World War II.

"All of our guys are veterans, so we know what it means to be a veteran," said Trent Tallman, a handler with the team who likes to incorporate a history lesson of sorts into his talks, describing how the duties of the dogs who served alongside the veterans differed from those of today's canine soldiers.

"It's neat to see the energy and it's good for us too," Tallman said. "Sometimes you get an audience that doesn't really seem to care, but not with this crowd. We want to stay as long as we can and make sure we answer every question."

And clearly, the intensity of the attention and interest from the audience is not lost on the dogs. "They feed a lot off of the crowd," said Tallman. "If they are cheering and clapping, then the dogs will be into it too. Nothing makes me prouder than when we get to go up in front of a group of veterans, especially World War II veterans."

6

STRESS RELIEF

No matter which branch they hail from, it's no secret that many members of the military are not comfortable with opening up or admitting that they're struggling emotionally as a result of the stress and pressure of their jobs and missions, whether they're serving stateside or deployed to a war zone. No surprise, since military training has traditionally emphasized that its soldiers keep a stiff upper lip and not show any emotion.

"Everybody is stressed in a war zone," said Col. David D. Rabb of California, and unit commander for the 113th Combat Stress Control Detachment based in Garden Grove, California. "The question is, how are you going to deal with it? Stress is a silent enemy. It will take you out."

The one thing that can break the façade and help soldiers to deal with stress often comes in the form of a fellow service member, albeit with four legs, not two, and covered with fur. When military therapists and psychologists watched as some of the most battle-hardened warriors immediately softened up in the presence of a canine soldier, it wasn't difficult for them to figure that perhaps a four-legged official "therapist" could succeed where a human counterpart had previously failed. Indeed, even the stray dogs that roam around farflung military bases have worked wonders in easing the rigors of deployed life.

And so during the war in Iraq, the military began to recruit canine therapy dogs to serve in war zones specifically to help provide emotional comfort and solace.

Even though many of these dogs come from breeds other than the muscular teeth-baring bite-suit-attacking German shepherds and Belgian Malinois that make up the majority of the military's canine elite, they still have to go through a similarly rigorous training program, according to Army Capt. Theresa Schillreff, an occupational therapist with the 254th Combat Outpatient Stress Clinic, who worked in Afghanistan alongside a yellow Lab named Major Timmy. "He has been trained to deal with the stress that a dog would endure here," she said. "For example, he's been out to firing ranges and has practice getting on and off helicopters with all his safety gear on, including ear muffs and safety goggles."

ZEKE

A black Labrador retriever named Zeke — with an official rank of Sgt. 1st Class — traveled throughout northern Iraq for two years to bring comfort to thousands of military personnel alongside his human counterpart, Spc. Lawrence Shipman, a patient administrative specialist with the 85th Medical Combat Stress Control Detachment. Shipman marveled at his canine partner's talent for melting even the most war-hardened soldier.

"Zeke is like an ice-breaker," said Shipman. "Sometimes people are scared to talk to us, but when they see the therapy dog, soldiers naturally come up to pet him and generally loosen up. Then, most of the time, we are able to talk about anything that is possibly bothering them."

After returning home from Iraq, Shipman wanted Zeke to retire so he

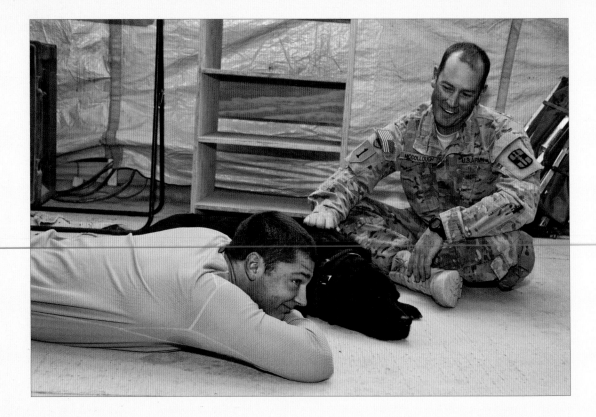

could adopt him, but as is often the case, the Army had other plans. Sgt. 1st Class Zeke calmly accepted his new mission with new handler, Sgt. Paul McCollough, and subsequently headed for Afghanistan. "There are a lot of dog lovers in the military, and whenever Zeke comes around it's almost like everyone is just not 'here' for a few minutes," said McCollough. "They're with their dog back home and away from the stressors they have to deal with in this environment."

In fact, Zeke has been so effective at his job that in 2011 he was inducted into the Order of the Spur, a military organization that honors soldiers who have gone above and beyond the call of duty to serve their fellow soldiers.

MAJOR EDEN

The dogs who make it into the MWD elite corps are the cream of the crop; only a small percentage of those who complete training for explosive or drug detection ever make it into the field to work side by side with a human handler.

Canines can wash out of training for a variety of reasons, but one red Lab who flunked out for essentially being too affectionate and sweet happily went on to succeed in another program that fit her personality to a T: therapy dog.

Along with her human partner, Pfc. Alex Fanning, a behavioral health specialist with the 98th Medical Detachment, Major Eden was deployed to Afghanistan in 2013. From the moment they hit the ground they were attracting attention. It didn't take much: Fanning and Eden often just walked around the base and within minutes soldiers would naturally gravitate towards them,

Major Eden serves as a magnet, collecting soldiers as they walk by.

"Our job is to travel around Bagram and to other Forward Operating Bases where members of the 98th are located," explained Fanning. "We tell people who we are, what we do and what we can do for them. At the same

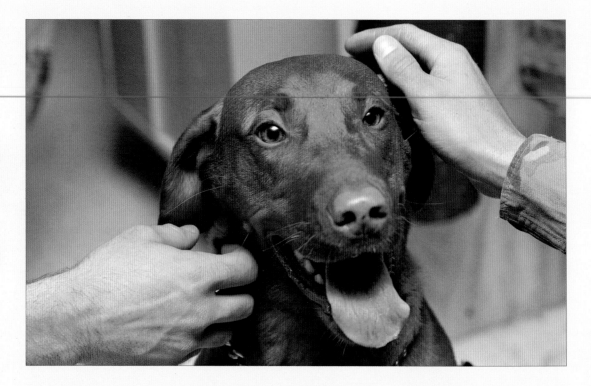

time we let them play with Eden, which brings people to us instead of me just going to them.

"She also helps us get a foot in the door with people because she puts smiles on faces," he explained. "Then we tell them what we offer and how we can help them out."

Eden also sits in on individual and group therapy sessions. Fanning regularly conducts a three-day program where soldiers can take a break and talk with a group of therapists about the stress of deployment, pressure from family

back home, or anything else they like. Again, Major Eden plays a big role in helping troops to open up, and Fanning has witnessed major breakthroughs with the soldiers he's worked with. Happily, his own higher-ups have seen it, too. "I've talked with generals and colonels who are just so on board with the program," said Fanning. "They see the difference we make in their soldiers and how happy it makes them. It's a great feeling to work where I do, watching the troops come in and get the help they need to perform their jobs and knowing we're really making a difference."

MAJOR TIMMY

Another combat stress dog who followed in the pawprints of Sgt. 1st Class Zeke and Major Eden in Afghanistan is a yellow Lab named Major Timmy, who was so good at his job that he was promoted from staff sergeant after only two years of service.

Major Timmy is part of the 528th Medical Detachment's combat stress control team. Shortly after he arrived to serve at Bagram Airfield in Afghanistan, soldiers and staff came to expect they could always toss a ball or hug a furry neck when they needed a mental health break.

Army Capt. Christine Beck served as Timmy's handler in his first two years of deployment, and she saw firsthand the almost instantaneous effect that Timmy had on a soldier in a state of shock who had watched as a friend died in front of him. "You could tell in his face that he was still in that numb

state," said Beck. But then he got down on the floor to pet Timmy. "I thought he was going to pet the fur off of him. I could see his face soften up and I could see him almost come out of that state. Then, he started talking about the event and started talking about how hard it was and what a rough week it had been."

For Spc. Aerick Gomez, a signal support specialist with the 313th Joint Movement Control Battalion, it didn't take long for him to be convinced of Timmy's therapeutic talents. "Seeing Timmy gives me a sense of home," he said. "Timmy is definitely a morale booster. Being able to pet a dog is not the everyday norm in Afghanistan."

Beck concurs. "The act of petting a dog helps relieve stress," she said. "Service members play with him, talk to him, or just throw a ball around for a while. It's a touch from home." And while soldiers themselves can be reluctant to reach out for help, the same goes for their commanders. "Many times, a

commander won't call for preventative [stress relief] services for their team, but they will call for a Timmy visit."

Beck reports that one soldier informed her that under normal circumstances he refused to set foot within one hundred meters of her office, but that he made an exception for Major Timmy. "Sometimes they will pet Timmy and talk to Timmy without ever really looking at me," she said. "But that's okay because they are getting some outlet and talking to someone."

LUGNUT

While therapy dogs like Major Timmy and Sgt. 1st Class Zeke deploy to military bases around the world and provide an invaluable service to troops and staff overseas, there's another group that employs dogs in a special way: they greet those who are returning from often lengthy deployments and usually wondering how they're going to make the transition upon returning home.

Though he lacks an official title, a golden retriever named Lugnut serves an important purpose: as part of the Indianapolis-based group Welcome Home Dogs, Lugnut and his owner, dog trainer Kristi Rush, regularly show up at Camp Atterbury to greet soldiers who are returning from long and possibly traumatic stints overseas. Rush and Lugnut work in several different ways. First, along with a few other dog-and-handler pet-therapy teams from around the area, they'll show up at the airport to greet soldiers once they first set foot on American soil again. Next, they'll visit troops who are being demobilized and debriefed while they stay on the base, a process that can often take a week or more and involve numerous examinations to evaluate their physical and mental health as well as filling out mountains of paperwork.

Just like soldiers deployed overseas who smile and visibly relax in the presence of Timmy and Zeke, when Lugnut makes his rounds with the returning troops they exhale and offer up a few smiles. They may even begin to open up a little, telling their stories to a goofy-looking golden retriever with a funny name.

Rush launched Welcome Home Dogs in 2010 because she wanted to share her love for dogs and give something back to local soldiers who had served. "After I've witnessed what our dogs can offer to these soldiers who have just come back from overseas, to see them relax and smile and feel the love, my goal has become to get as many teams on board as possible so that we could reach as many of our soldiers as possible," said Rush. After Lugnut was certified as a therapy dog, Rush started to spread the word to as many dog lovers as she could so she could help even more soldiers. Soon she had six teams certified and ready to contribute.

"I knew immediately that we were a success when I saw the look on the soldiers' faces," she said. "They begin to smile. Their bodies shift more in their chairs and their posture becomes more relaxed. They open up and start to talk about their dogs, past, present and future. Hope pours out of them into the dogs and the dogs just swallow it up without question. It never fails to warm my heart to watch our dogs in action."

★★★ (7) ★★★
AT YOUR SERVICE

MWDs aren't the only canines who are selflessly helping active-duty military personnel; sometimes a furry therapist is one of the best ways to help speed recovery and build a new life outside the military.

A wide variety of canines are doing their part to help injured servicemen and -women to recover, as well as allow disabled and retired veterans to lead more fulfilling lives out in the real world.

SHAMUS

When Marine veteran Kyle Reid was deployed to Afghanistan in March of 2011 as a landing support specialist, he had no idea what to expect. And later, when he returned home, he wasn't sure how to ease back into civilian life, but that was OK with his wife, Andee; she was just glad to get her husband back in one piece.

But it soon became clear that something wasn't right. Though Kyle tried to hide his emotional pain and refused to talk about what he had witnessed,

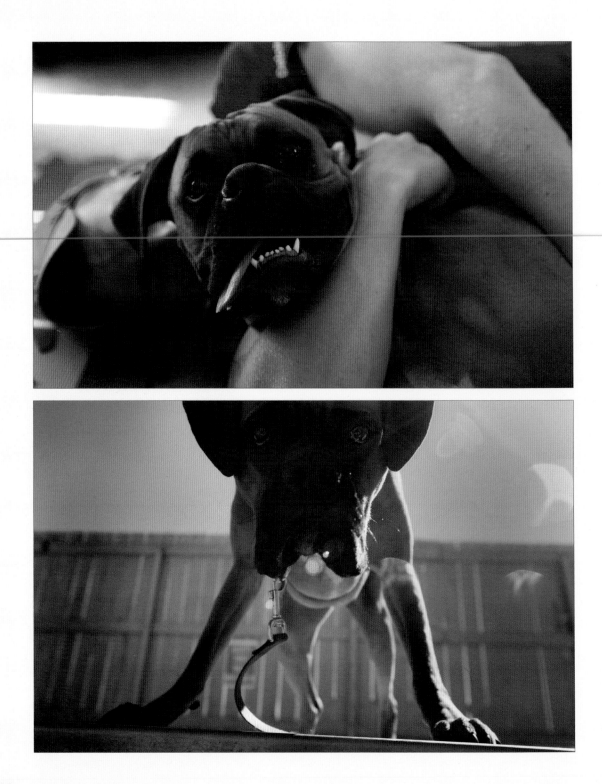

his body couldn't hide from the trauma he had seen: through night terrors and hallucinations, his body and mind were both telling him that something was dreadfully wrong.

And then came the seizures. "If I get too stressed or anxious, my body

decides to hit the reset button," he said. "My eyes roll, I convulse, and I'm unresponsive."

In time, Kyle was experiencing as many as three seizures every day. Both he and Andee were at their wits' end when one of Kyle's physicians mentioned that a specially trained service dog might be able to alert to an oncoming seizure and even help to prevent seizures in the first case. They were intrigued, but instead of waiting to receive a service dog from one of the many organizations out there, a process that could take up to a year or more, Kyle and Andee instead thought that their own dog, a boxer named Shamus, could do the job.

The three got started right away. First they trained Shamus to become familiar with Kyle's heartbeat—both at rest and when a seizure is looming. Then Shamus took over and trained Kyle to recognize the signs of an impending seizure so he could take active steps to calm himself down. "When I'm getting stressed or anxious, Shamus will lay his head on my lap, lay at my feet or put his paw on me," he said. "That reminds me that I need to try and calm myself down before it gets too bad and I do seize."

The impact that Shamus has had on the family has been striking. Not only have Kyle's seizures dropped in frequency and severity, but he also entered the Marine Corps Trials, a series of paralympic races for wounded and disabled Marines, where he competed in events in track and swimming. All the while during training and the competition itself, Shamus never left Kyle's side, where he remained vigilant, looking for signs of stress and also serving as a cheerleader and a welcome reminder of how far Kyle had progressed. "Shamus doesn't get in the pool with me and he doesn't run on the track with me, but I'm always within view so he knows what I'm doing," Kyle said.

JAMES

A golden retriever named James doesn't know it, but he's part of a program at Walter Reed National Military Medical Center that gives back to injured and traumatized service members in two ways: First, disabled and injured service members are training him to become a service dog. Second, after his training is over, he will go on to live with another disabled soldier, where he will work as a service dog.

"We help them with [increasing] socialization and emotional regulation while reducing their sense of isolation," said Carolyn Ford, who helps guide the members training the dogs, and adds that the process of training the dogs actually helps the veterans to recover more quickly. "Many times wounded warriors will go to appointments and then go back to their rooms, isolating themselves, and [the dogs help] . . . get them out and get them active."

The dogs learn to carry out a variety of tasks, from opening the refrigerator and grabbing a bottle of water to opening and closing doors and even switching on and off lights, standard tasks that a service dog must know how to do. The trainers are also responsible for grooming their dogs and carrying

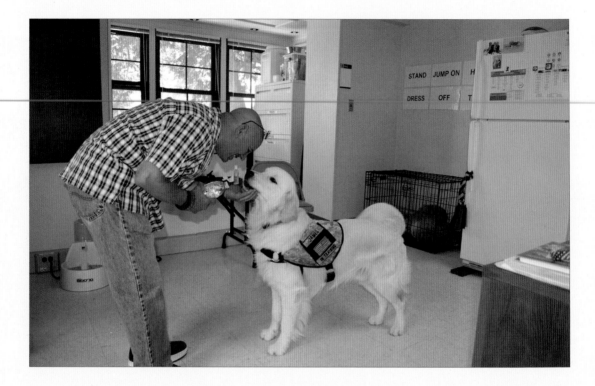

out other necessary hygiene, including brushing the dogs' teeth, clipping their nails, and also learning to be aware of cues the dogs may be throwing off if they're not feeling well and need to go to the vet.

Col. Matthew St. Laurent, chief of occupational therapy at Walter Reed, helps run the program and says he's seen it work miracles on the veterans, helping to ease trauma, depression, anxiety, and stress. "I can tell them that I can't erase their past experiences, but maybe I can provide them some tools for living by inviting them to train a dog for a fellow vet," he said.

The veterans also teach the dogs to focus on performing a particular task while tuning out disruptions so they can do their work. At the same time, emotionally traumatized veterans must learn how to do a similar thing for themselves: to regulate their own emotions and behavior and keep them in check so they, too, can concentrate on the task at hand.

"A dog in training may not respond to you if you display a depressive tone," said St. Laurent. "A dog attends to affection and loves when you cheer it on."

"There's more to the program than just the socialization piece," said Emily Mittelman, a service dog instructor at Walter Reed. "A participant can learn emotional regulation by shifting their voice to do the correct tones for commands or praise. They are essentially re-training the way they think about talking to people and dogs."

In 2014, S.Sgt. Steven Betancourt, a logistics specialist, was severely injured in Afghanistan, and after being left with a spinal injury and other physical problems he had what seemed like a perfect excuse to wallow in misery. "Learning how to adapt when you're healing is a whole complicated process, dealing with changes and how to go on with your future," he admitted. But then came an invitation to help train the dogs, and it wasn't long until he was signing up for extra hours to work with them. After a couple of hours of training sessions with James, Betancourt's whole demeanor and outlook shifts.

"When I come to work with the dogs my frame of mind changes and I have a great time," he said. "When I leave, I'm happy and smiling and everything becomes very calm."

Though some of his fellow trainers don't have physical injuries, Betancourt says that his own physical limitations are a huge plus in training James and the other dogs in the program who will likely go on to work with veterans who also have mobility issues. "I'm not able to walk like the average person anymore because I have a limp, and due to the spine injury, I'll never run again," he said. "So I have the dog walk at my pace, which is not the average person's pace. The dog has to learn how to adjust to me. But James will be able to help someone else with my condition because he's programmed to walk at a certain pace. It's great to be able to help a wounded warrior in that way."

PRISON PUPPIES

There's another military training program that uses soldiers to raise service dogs, but it's a bit of a shift from James. Instead of using disabled veterans to train dogs, this program uses service members who are serving time at the Naval Consolidated Brig aboard Marine Corps Air Station Miramar in San Diego to put service dogs in training through their paces.

Canine Companions for Independence is an organization that trains service dogs for disabled people all over the country, including soldiers who have been wounded in combat. They saw the clear need for more service dogs to live with and assist veterans, so when an opportunity to team up with the military to help train more dogs arose it didn't matter that the trainers had hit a few rough spots in the past. Actually, the fact that prisoners were available to spend eighteen months to train the dogs—with admittedly few distractions from the outside world—was a big plus.

"This is a win-win situation," said Cath Phillips, a dog trainer who teaches

in the prison program. "We have people here who have obviously done wrong. They want to turn their lives around, and they're doing it by loving the puppies for eighteen months and then sending the puppy on its way to do something for somebody else."

Indeed, prisoners in the program quickly realize that spending hours each day with their dog is life changing. "I wanted to come into the program initially because I thought it would be pretty fantastic just to have a dog around," said a prisoner. "What I found out after doing it for a while is I was able to give back

and help someone. You're bringing something positive out of the most negative experience of your life. You know that you're making something good happen."

There's a similar program at Joint Base Lewis-McChord in Washington State, and volunteer Veronica Quezada, who works as a parole clerk at the base, said the puppies have worked wonders in terms of boosting spirits around the base.

"Most of the guys here have been separated from their families for quite some time and just seeing the furry little guys walking around raises morale," she said. "Some of the prisoners look at this as a way to give back to the com-

munity. When they are in here they can't really do a lot to repay for what their actions have cost them, so it's a way to sort of make amends for some of the things that they have done."

"The program gives the people who are going to be in a facility for a long period of time a companion," said one inmate. "For me, it's a good stress reliever because you can always go to him and he'll be there."

And while the puppies obviously provide the inmates with an important job, their mere presence on base helps everyone who comes into contact with them.

"The dogs just bring out the best in people," said another inmate. "There are always smiles when the dog is around."

DINO

When Marine S.Sgt. Christopher Diaz, a dog handler based at the Marine Corps Air Ground Combat Center in Twentynine Palms, California, was killed in action in 2011 while serving in Afghanistan, his fellow handlers were not at all taken aback that Dino, his canine partner, steadfastly refused to work with another handler. They had seen their fair share of MWDs suffering after the loss of their partners, so Dino was sent back to his home base, where his colleagues thought some time off would help the grieving canine.

"When he first got back, I think it clicked in his head that Staff Sgt. Diaz wasn't coming back," said Sgt. Jonathan Overland, a dog handler at the base. "All I can remember hearing was that no one could [work with] . . . him. He became aggressive and didn't like anybody because they weren't Staff Sgt. Diaz."

Diaz's father, Salvador, wasn't surprised. "Before Dino, Chris had another dog named Waldo, and their relationship was the same as any other dog handler," said Diaz. But once Chris was paired up with Dino, it was clear that their partnership was meant to be.

"When Chris would talk about Dino or explain what he was doing with

him, his face would light up," said Diaz. "It was like when you have a passion for something whether it has to do with cars or motorcycles or even cooking, your face lights up with joy whenever you talk about it."

So when Dino refused to move on, Salvador came up with what he thought

was an ideal solution. He knew that dogs like Dino who could no longer serve were often adopted out to either handlers or civilians. What if he adopted Dino? After all, the dog served as a connection to his late son.

The adoption was finalized on June 7, 2014, and everyone agreed that it was one good thing to come out of a tragic situation. "Dino means love," said Diaz. "The reason I say love is because Dino has something of our son, just as Chris had something of him. The first time I met Dino, I stared at him and I actually saw Chris. Maybe it's just me, or maybe it's the mind at work, but I saw my son. Dino will be a part of the family. He's going to be everywhere

with us and be included in everything because it will be almost like having Chris again."

MUSH!

Perhaps one of the most effective ways for a battle-scarred warrior to start to recover is to get physical. At the very least, it can serve as a welcome distraction from the personal demons that often surface after a long, difficult deployment.

Getting physically active while surrounded by a crowd of boisterous, joyful canines was the impetus behind Jennifer Casillo's decision to launch a program to help retired service members venture into the outdoors in Alaska and learn to lead a team of sled dogs through the magnificent wilderness.

Casillo, a major with the Alaska Air National Guard who has also served with the Air Force and Air Force Reserve, saw firsthand how being on active duty can affect a man or woman, whether it's physical or psychological.

Along with her husband, Rick, who has competed in the Iditarod, Casillo runs Battle Dawgs Racing, a sled dog racing kennel in Big Lake, Alaska. Her group teamed up with Alaska's Healing Hearts, a nonprofit group that provides a wealth of opportunities for soldiers and their families to enjoy Alaska, includ-

ing hunting and fishing trips as well as dogsledding.

"The true battle for a veteran begins when they get home," Casillo said. "We dedicated the kennel to providing a platform to expose warriors to therapeutic and exciting experiences by harnessing the natural splendor of Alaska's landscape and the power of sled dogs."

"It's a perfect relationship," said Jessy Lakin, an Army combat veteran who now works at Alaska's Healing Hearts. Like Casillo, Lakin has witnessed the power that dogs can have on a warrior who's struggling, and adds that just watching the dogs work together when pulling a load can help a veteran take

some comfort from being part of a team, which is essentially how he lived while on active duty.

"The strength of a dog team is insane," said Lakin. "You have sixteen dogs pulling a sled with five-hundred pounds and dragging it over a thousand miles. If you put a warrior who is struggling around these dogs for ten minutes, the one-on-one connection that forms is just unbelievable."

Casillo agrees. "I love it when I can spend a whole day in the dog yard, it just clears my mind," she said. "We witness this in our warriors. They are able to let everything fall away for a while and are able to bond with the dogs and our team."

ISSAC

Indeed, retired Army captain Leslie Smith is a clear example of how much a service dog can add to the life of a disabled veteran, regardless of who trains the canine. While she was serving in Bosnia in 2002, she contracted a blood disorder that resulted in the loss of her left leg and sight in her left eye. She was already considering getting a service dog, but when the eyesight in her right eye started to deteriorate she was declared legally blind and, shortly after, a yellow Lab named Issac arrived and gave her back her life.

"The day I got Issac," said Smith, "I felt like a child on Christmas. I thought to myself, there's my dog, he'll help me. Whenever I would cry, Issac would walk up and lick away my tears, and I knew everything was going to be okay."

Today Smith travels extensively to promote organizations that include the Wounded Warrior Project and Disabled Sports USA, and she points to her dog as the primary reason she is able to maintain a rigorous travel schedule. "Issac has given me the freedom and strength to continue my life," she said.

★ ★ ★ (8) ★ ★ ★

SECOND ACTS

When it's time for canine soldiers to retire, some head right for a well-deserved cushy life devoted to rest and relaxation and a few leisure activities while others find a pursuit where they can give back to others but that still allows for a good chunk of leisure time.

Just like their human companions do. But one difference is that because most military working dogs have had extensive aggression training, all soon-to-be-retired canines soldier must be thoroughly tested and screened before they can be adopted out. Of course, any non-handlers who wish to adopt them must also go through a similar testing process.

Before the year 2000, military working dogs who retired were required to be euthanized as a matter of course; the government believed the dogs were deemed unsuitable for living in a home situation with a family, and by the age of nine or ten many of the dogs also suffered from chronic health problems that are common in MWDs. "A lot of these dogs have joint issues and other aches and pains because they have been working their whole lives," said Daniel

Heinzig, an operations sergeant with the 504th Military Police Battalion at Joint Base Lewis-McChord. "They've put a lot on the line and have risked their lives for us. The least we can do is give them a home."

Despite the potential hurdles, most would maintain that these dogs deserved a happy retirement no matter what. Thankfully, the future of canine soldiers changed in 2000 when Congress passed "Robby's Law," named for the MWD who inspired the legislation that would green-light retired dogs for adoption—previous handlers get first dibs before members of the general public—provided the canine passes a number of tests, which include aggression exercises, veterinarian reports on the dog's health, and also personal recommendations from previous handlers and kennel masters who can vouch for the dog's character. One thing is certain: everyone is gunning for the dog to live the life of Riley in retirement.

"It means a lot to me," said Pfc. Jared Bridges, a dog handler with the 510th MP Detachment at Fort Campbell, Kentucky. "They work their entire lives here, working hard days, long hours, and deploy multiple times. It'd be nice to just go see them get a couch somewhere and just relax and live the good life of an actual dog."

SATO

Some dogs who retire mid-career do so because of medical problems. When he was just five years old, a Belgian Malinois named Sato started to limp on his regular rounds as a bomb dog alongside his handler, Tech. Sgt. Ashley-Marie Umstead. Like many dog handler teams, Umstead and Sato—whose home base was the 10th Security Forces Squadron at the Air Force Academy in Colorado—spent so much time together that they were keenly aware of minute changes in each other's physical or emotional state.

While they were deployed to Qatar their bond only grew. "I was away from my six-month-old daughter, and Sato was like my counselor and best friend," Umstead said. "I told him everything, and he would sit with me and

look at me like, 'I love you.' "

Umstead knew that Sato's days as a crackerjack detection dog were quickly drawing to a close, but she realized he could still serve his fellow soldiers, only in a different capacity. "He was too young to stay at home without eating my

couch," she said. So after she adopted him she set about finding a retirement job for him that would suit his temperament. She occasionally brought him to her office at the Academy, where she worked as a flight chief, and she had already realized from their regular rounds around the base that Sato enjoyed interacting with other soldiers and civilian employees, serving as a kind of unofficial therapy dog. It wasn't unusual for colleagues and visitors to stop by her office several times a day just to get in a few pets and scratches.

"He's a good asset to have here every day," said Airman 1st Class Khari Berry, an entry controller with the squad. "He's usually happy-go-lucky and a good stress reliever after a hard day."

But Umstead wanted to make things official as well as expand Sato's reach, so she signed up for a program with Therapy Dogs International so that Sato could become certified and they could go off base to visit people at hospitals, rehabilitation centers, and other health facilities.

"I'd like to work with wounded warriors because I can tell them that Sato was in the military, he deployed and is now medically retired," she said. "It gives them some rapport to connect and I think it makes the relationship more special.

"I enjoy seeing people forget their cares for a couple minutes when they're with Sato," she added. "Sato doesn't judge. He doesn't care what you've done or what you're going to do, he just wants to spend that moment in time with you. That's all he wants and all he has to do."

CARLY

The attack was a total blur.

On that fateful day in April of 2012 near Kandahar Airfield in Afghanistan, even though most of his left leg had disappeared in the IED blast, the only thing S.Sgt. Brian Williams could think of was his canine partner, Carly. Where was his dog and was he okay?

When Williams heard that Carly had escaped injury, only then could he focus on his own pain and recovery. He was airlifted to Walter Reed National Military Medical Center in Bethesda, Maryland, for surgery and rehab, while Carly was transported back to their home base of Joint Base McGuire-Dix-Lakehurst in New Jersey. Whenever colleagues from his own 87th Security Forces Squadron came to visit him and expressed concern for his injuries as well as good wishes for his recovery, he always brushed them off.

"Every time we went down to visit Brian, his first question was always 'How is Carly?' said S.Sgt. Allison Price, a dog handler with the squadron. And so on one of the next visits they decided to bring Carly along to surprise both of them.

"The first time we brought Carly down to see him, he jumped into his lap and started licking his face," said Price. "Carly never forgot who his dad is. They truly have an unbreakable bond."

They continued to bring Carly on visits to the medical center, but instead of getting easier, it got harder. Price said that with each visit Carly had an increasingly hard time leaving Brian. One day, Carly simply refused to leave Brian's side, barking and crying. About the same time, Brian was getting ready to leave the hospital and head home, but he realized he was going to need some help getting around and managing on a daily basis.

That's when the lightbulb went off: Why couldn't Carly be his service dog?

The seed was planted, and happily, about eighteen months after Williams was injured in Afghanistan, with a little bit of string pulling, Carly was officially retired from the military and began his new career as a service dog.

IVY

When Stephen Heath, a dog handler with the U.S. Marines, first set eyes on his new canine partner in 2010, he would have been the first to admit that he was less than impressed. After all, he was expecting a big, burly male German shepherd or

Belgian Malinois. After all, that's what most of the other handlers he knew had.

He got a surprise when he was introduced to Ivy, a slightly built black Lab, significantly smaller than the other newly assigned canine partners and a different breed besides, not one known for being particularly ferocious.

Not to mention, she was female.

But orders were orders, so he and his specialized bomb-detection dog headed off to Afghanistan for a seven-month deployment in Helmand Province. Despite his initial misgivings, Heath said that he became attached to Ivy in a matter of days, and vice versa. Indeed, it was a rare moment when they were separated. "She was my companion, my best friend, and she protected me, too," he said. "We were like family."

When Heath's deployment ended he headed back to the United States, but Ivy had several more years to go, so she teamed up with another handler.

Heath was determined: he planned to adopt Ivy when her contract was up. Ivy was a Contract Working Dog, or CWD, owned by a private company that raises and trains detection dogs before hiring them out to the military for a specific period of time.

When Ivy's term was up in 2014, she arrived back at the company's facility in Virginia and the contractor got in touch with Heath to see if he still wanted to take her, with one catch: Heath would have to pay her way to Houston, where he lived with his fiancée. He told the contractor yes, of course, he wanted Ivy and hung up the phone. He started to research different possibilities for transport, and that's when he discovered a nonprofit organization right in Houston called Mission K9 Rescue, which helps rescue and find new homes for retired working dogs as well as reuniting them with previous handlers.

After a couple of phone calls, it was finalized: Ivy and Heath would be reunited.

TORA

Though handlers and their canine partners are joined at the hip more often than not, the truth is that this attachment can create more than its fair share of frustration and stubbornness between the two sides, in good times and bad. But like many equally close human partnerships, it's often the more contentious relationships that end up forging bonds that can be closer and more inti-

mate than anything else in life.

"You grow to love your dog because of the amount of time and effort spent with them," said Tech. Sgt. Gabriel Travers, a handler with the 31st Security Forces Squadron out of Aviano Air Base in Italy. "Then there are times when the dog is telling you 'No, I'm not going to do it today,' and they frustrate you to no end."

When Travers completed handler training and teamed up with his first canine partner, a narcotics-detection dog named Fuels, they worked well together and respected each other and the dog performed his job admirably, though his aggressive tendencies were pretty much nonexistent. It wasn't until Travers was transferred to Italy and was teamed up with an explosive-detection dog named Tora that he realized how close such a partnership could become, in part because his new canine partner was so different. Unlike Fuels, Tora was

so aggressive and contrary that she fought both Travers and others at the base on absolutely everything, like a small child who was constantly questioning everything in her path.

Travers was initially aggravated by his new partner's temperament in part because she continually challenged him. After all, when Tora fought him Travers had to shift his own approach and outlook in order to convince the dog to do what *he* wanted her to do, which even included eating and sleeping.

Soon, however, Travers came to appreciate Tora's orneriness and revel in the closeness of the partnership. In fact, he began to regard his canine companion in the same way he would view—and protect—a family member. In 2012 they deployed to Afghanistan, and after a short adjustment period they began to go on regular patrols outside the wire. As time passed, the dangers increased, and soon Tora began to rebel. "There was a time when we were in too many firefights and she didn't want to work anymore," he said. "She was mentally done after being so close to explosions. All I could do was to try and ask her to put her life on the line for me and let her know I'd protect her."

As a result of Tora's reluctance—and the increasing peril—Travers took a cue from his dog and he began to question things as well, asking himself, *How can I ask her to do it again?* "If you're scared to walk outside the wire, the dog can sense that and they're not going to work efficiently," said Travers.

However, the end of their deployment was still months away and he felt he and Tora owed the soldiers they were protecting their best efforts. So once again, he shifted his mind-set to accommodate his canine partner, which, in turn, helped ease Tora's anxieties, and she eventually became a little more relaxed whenever they went out on patrol. "At the end of the day in those environments, we loved each other and survived through it together. She's more than a dog, she is like my child," said Travers.

When their deployment was over, they headed back to Italy and worked together for three more years until it was time for Tora to retire. Travers adopted her, and his wife, Megan, and their two sons welcomed Tora as a member of their family.

"I look at her not only as a dog, but as a person who saved my husband's life," said Megan Travers. "I respect and love Tora, because I know what they've been through."

BERNIE

Traditionally, handlers get first dibs on adopting a military working dog who was their partner. If there are no takers, the dog is offered up to a specially screened and pre-approved member of the general public, who's probably been on a lengthy waiting list for months, if not years.

But sometimes the dog is so popular that the handlers have to draw straws to see who gets the honor of adopting the soon-to-be-retired canine soldier. In that case, the dog's last handler typically gains precedence.

That's just what happened with an MWD named Bernie, a Belgian Malinois based out of the Marine Corps air station in Yuma, Arizona. In fact, Bernie was so well loved by her handlers that several had already made it clear that they wanted to adopt her, setting the stage for a fight. But in the end, Cpl. Bret Reynolds, her last handler and the one who'd spent two-and-a-half years with her, won out.

"Every handler dreams of this, to be able to adopt a dog they've handled," he said.

As things turned out, Reynolds left the Marine Corps shortly after Bernie retired, and he happily reported that his former canine partner had no trouble adjusting to the relative cushiness of retirement. For one, the dog has already mastered the art of maneuvering her way onto the bed to sleep with Reynolds and his wife.

But neither one particularly minds.

"Trusting her with my life is one of the biggest commitments I've ever made," said Reynolds. "Trusting someone who doesn't speak, who can't tell you what she feels, trusting her with my life on bomb threat calls has been huge and something I'll always take with me. Besides, she's the only girl I'm allowed to love other than my wife."

★★★ (9) ★★★
STAND DOWN

Though they were once quite rare, retirement ceremonies for Military Working Dogs—whether after a long, full life of service or when a canine soldier's career is prematurely ended due to a medical issue or PTSD—are quickly spreading throughout all branches of the U.S. military.

Just like two-legged veterans, MWDs who retire are honored by their colleagues and typically enjoy a party, a formal retirement send-off, and a good meal.

"A retirement ceremony is just as appropriate for our canines as it is for airmen who serve faithfully all the way up until they are eligible to retire," said Maj. Douglas Whitehead, commander of the 355th Security Force Squadron at Davis-Monthan Air Force Base in Arizona. "It's a thrill where I actually get to do a retirement ceremony for an MWD, because unfortunately, more often than not, I am doing a memorial service for one of them."

Whether or not MWDs are awarded a Purple Heart or Bronze Star for their faithful service, former handlers and soldiers alike regard each and every canine soldier to be a hero beyond measure. And many of them strive to show up for the retirement ceremony if it's at all humanly possible. One explosive-detection dog named Desant—shown in the photograph enjoying his retirement cake—was honored for his service as part of the 100th Air Refueling

Wing at the RAF Mildenhall base in the United Kingdom. Desant had a remarkable career, clocking over nine thousand hours actively spent on the job, where he worked alongside seven different handlers. He also helped the Secret Service on security details to clear rooms for former First Ladies and Presidents.

"Desant is a dog with a lot of character—he's really affectionate and goofy," said Debbie Black, a kennel attendant at RAF Mildenhall, who cared for Desant, and laughed as she remembered how he hated having his picture taken and having his toenails clipped and always had a problem going to the vet. "He has to have two muzzles on, is constantly growling at them, and tries to bite them whenever the opportunity occurs. But he's mellowed a lot since he's no longer doing regimented training any more—he just wants to be loved—but he'll still bite if given the chance."

It's no wonder, then, that about fifty people showed up at his retirement ceremony—but probably not the base veterinarian—to celebrate a job well done and to swap stories about their time spent alongside the much-loved canine soldier.

TANJA

When a canine soldier named Tanja, based with the 366th Security Forces Squadron at Mountain Home Air Force Base in Idaho, retired in early 2013, she had a record of outstanding service behind her, deploying five times over her career and winning the loyalty of her numerous handlers.

But there was one additional distinction that she had that no other MWD had earned at the time that she stepped down:

Tanja was the longest-serving MWD throughout the entire Department of Defense, including all branches of the military as well as the Secret Service

and other security details. The Belgian Malinois had actively served her country for almost twelve years, a fact that didn't surprise a couple of her handlers. Tech. Sgt. Roseann Kelly, Tanja's last handler, marveled at the dog's stamina at an age when other canine soldiers would be lagging. "After all these years, she was still kicking butt," said Kelly.

S.Sgt. Robert Wilson also worked with Tanja and recalled how her perseverance led to deterring bad guys on patrol and discovering explosives on routine sweeps, but also one day when she helped discover a secret cache of classified documents that had fallen into the wrong hands. "One time while we were deployed, she located explosive devices inside a vehicle," said Wilson. "However, upon further search of the vehicle we found stolen classified documents hidden inside. In a roundabout way, she was able to alert us of potential explosives and keep extremely valuable classified information safe."

Both Kelly and Wilson mentioned that Tanja had stood out among other canine soldiers for her even temperament. "I could go on all day about Tanja because she is a terrific dog and I consider it an honor to have been able to work with her," said Wilson. "I never had any issues working with her and she was definitely the best dog I have ever had."

For her part, Kelly admired and respected her canine partner so much—dressing Tanja in sweaters on cold nights, for instance—that the other handlers teased her. "I actually babied her quite a bit," Kelly admitted, but she justified playing dress-up with Tanja because the base veterinarian had told her that the circulation in most older dogs slows down with age. "I wanted to ensure she was cozy and warm during the cold winters," Kelly said.

Kelly didn't expect Tanja to have much trouble downshifting to retired life. "She's been preparing and practicing for house-dog life for years," Kelly said. "She loves to lounge around and play games like most dogs do. As old as she is she continues to have a fantastic personality and endless spunk. She has served her country and can now look forward to enjoying herself and relaxing."

KOBUS

Like many handlers, Sgt. Holly Moore was amazed at how quickly the bond formed between herself and Kobus, a Dutch shepherd MWD assigned to be her partner in 2013. As a part of the canine soldier team with the 550th MWD Detachment out of Fort Bragg, Moore and Kobus were joined at the hip shortly after their first meeting.

"It was just an instant bond," Moore said.

Even others noticed how close they were. "They've only been together for about three and a half months, so we're really proud of the gains they've made

in such a short amount of time," said 1st Lt. Matthew Rowell, who oversees the dog and handler teams at the unit. Though part of the closeness of a team's bond is simply unexplainable, Moore thought that their connection was partly due to the fact that she believed that Kobus was capable of doing just about anything which she regularly conveyed to the dog.

"Whatever dog I think is the best, Kobus is going to be better than that," she said. "So when I leave here, Kobus is going to be the best dog and I know that [his next] handler better do good things with him."

After all, when she first signed up to be a dog handler, Moore regarded it to be her primary duty to protect the soldiers she was assigned to work with. "I want all the units, whoever we might get attached to, to feel safe and comfortable knowing that we'll take them back home," she said. "That's my job. I feel comfortable knowing that if me and Kobus are out there, we can save twenty lives behind us."

As it turned out, part of the reason why they were so fiercely attached was because of Kobus's temperament: when they were separated for any reason, for instance, if Moore went out on leave, the dog would become visibly depressed. In addition, while Kobus excelled at his training regimen and was normally very obedient, the only task he regularly struggled with was to keep his distance when she ordered a command for him to do so.

"Kobus needed me and whenever he couldn't see me, he would go nuts," Moore said. Indeed, when the pair was off duty Kobus would sit and stare at Moore with a goofy look on his face, something akin to a lovesick suitor.

When they deployed to Afghanistan on Veterans Day in 2013—her second deployment, his first—they became even closer, as is the case for most handler teams. Their deployment lasted just four months due to health issues for both, but when they returned to Fort Bragg they continued to serve by going on patrol and conducting explosive sweeps at the base and in the local community as well.

But then Kobus started to have trouble walking. He was diagnosed with a fast-developing cancer that couldn't be treated. The last night of the dog's life, Moore and fellow handlers held a vigil until morning. After Kobus was euthanized, Moore was devastated. "It was one of the hardest things I've ever dealt with," she said.

The next few days passed in a fog of grief and loss. But then Moore decided there was one tiny thing she could do to help. "I always told myself I'd never get a K-9 tattoo, and I never would have for any other dog," she said. "But the very next day, I got his paw print [and name] tattooed as close to my heart as I could, so I would always have part of him with me."

DAYSI

The cold, gray day at Joint Base San Antonio–Lackland in late February 2015 clearly matched the mood of the members of the 802nd Security Forces Squadron lining the sidewalk leading up to the Holland Military Working Dog Hospital, where they were getting ready to say good-bye to one of their own: Daysi, an MWD who had become certified in narcotics detection just one year earlier, had been diagnosed with an inoperable tumor. Today her colleagues were providing her with a hero's last salute.

Her handler, S.Sgt. Paul Olmos, held Daysi's leash as they slowly made their way towards the entrance, their pace a far cry from only a few months earlier when he struggled to keep up with his canine partner. "Daysi became one hell of a runner," Olmos said. "We ran though an obstacle course and up hills for a total of four miles. There were times when she dragged me up those hills. We became stronger together and I'll never forget that.

"Through all the training we've done together and the long twelve- to fourteen-hour days, it was just me and her," Olmos said. "She's my partner."

Their bond, like those of most MWD teams, was intense, but even more so because it was the first assignment for both. "Olmos was Daysi's first official handler and she was his first dog," said Tech. Sgt. Kevin Nelson, kennel master at the 802nd. "Their relationship was immense because this was their first

experience as an MWD team."

After the MWD team took a few more steps towards the hospital, Olmos was having trouble keeping his emotions in check. But then again, so was everyone else, whether they were saluting the canine soldier or flanking Olmos'

side. Each step brought them a few seconds closer to the inevitable sad truth of this day.

Just the previous month, trainers noticed that Daysi was having trouble walking; a veterinarian examined her left leg and determined that physical therapy might help. But after a few days she wasn't getting any better, and the doctor discovered a fast-growing inoperable tumor in her leg that was constricting a nerve, causing pain and immobility. Under the circumstances, there was only one procedure that could be prescribed: euthanasia. But first, Daysi's comrades would provide her with a procession by military police, sirens wailing as dozens of soldiers lined the walkway to offer up a final salute, as befitting any soldier.

"The news of Daysi's declining health hit us hard, this sort of news always does," Nelson said. "These dogs are our brothers and sisters in arms as well."

Other handlers at the base each took turns saying good-bye to Daysi.

When the team climbed the steps to the hospital, Olmos almost couldn't find the strength to open the door.

He paused, his hand on the door handle, and after taking a deep breath Olmos escorted his partner inside.

DIESEL AND DOBRYNYA

When the news first hit that terrorists had attacked Paris on November 13, 2015, people throughout the world were horrified at the senseless violence.

POLICE NATIONALE

Many anticipated an imminent retaliatory response against the members of the Islamic State who were found to be responsible for launching the attacks.

It should be no surprise that the French anti-terrorist police force known as Research, Assistance, Intervention, and Deterrence, or RAID—akin to the SWAT teams in the United States—brought with them a highly trained dog who would play a vital role in the ensuing search and counterterrorism raid.

Diesel, a Belgian Malinois, was seven years old and one of fifteen dogs who worked with the squad. He had served on the French force for five years when he accompanied his partner on the mission, entering a third-floor apart-

ment in the Paris suburb of Saint-Denis on November 18 to apprehend the suspects.

When it was all over, five suspected terrorists were in custody, the bodies of three others were found, and Diesel—who was scheduled to retire in the spring of 2016—had been killed.

People all over the world expressed their sadness and sympathy, and Twitter hashtags—#JeSuisChien and #JeSuisDiesel—soon began to appear on the social media site. Two weeks later, a group of Russian counterterrorism police held a ceremony at the French embassy in Moscow to present Dobrynya, a German shepherd puppy named after a Russian folk hero, to the RAID team. Though the Russians couldn't bring back Diesel, their gift of a puppy could help to bolster the morale of a battered city.

"The puppy you are giving us today will replace Diesel and proves your friendship," said Jean-Maurice Ripert, France's ambassador to Moscow. "They are waiting for this puppy in Paris."

Diesel's memory and the sacrifice he made were further honored in late 2015 when the People's Dispensary for Sick Animals, an animal charity based in Great Britain, posthumously awarded him with the Dickin Medal, an honor given to animals who have displayed extraordinary bravery and loyalty to duty during wartime and other conflicts.

"Following the tragic terrorist events in Paris last month, where many innocent people lost their lives, Diesel was instrumental in helping the French police locate and deal with the perpetrators," said PDSA Director General Jan McLoughlin. "Diesel is a truly deserving recipient. His gallant actions helped to protect human life in the face of imminent danger and we are very proud to honor him in this way."

DEXTER

At Davis-Monthan Air Force Base in Arizona, the first MWD retirement ceremony was held in 2014 to honor a German shepherd named Dexter, a member of the 355th Security Force Squadron, who was forced to retire because of a medical condition. Dexter was a much-valued member of the squad, serving for more than three years as a dual-purpose dog, excelling at both patrol duties and explosive detection.

Dexter deployed twice to the Middle East with his handler, S.Sgt. Alexandra Springman, despite a medical condition that caused his body temperature to fluctuate wildly when he was working, though after a brief rest it would stabilize. Some in the unit expressed their concern as to whether the dog was up to the task of protecting soldiers, but Springman maintained that Dexter would still be able to serve if they restricted their working hours to the night shift. Her commander agreed, and together the MWD team worked diligently to protect the troops both on the base and on patrol outside the wire.

"Dexter worked so fearlessly, diligently and all for the sake of pleasing me," Springman said. "These dogs don't understand the dangers behind their duties as MWDs, or the danger they put themselves in by working for us and protecting us, but to them it doesn't matter. They just want to hear 'good boy' or 'good girl' from their mom or dad and to play with their toys when they find the contraband they were trained to detect."

After Springman and Dexter's second deployment, it was determined that he should retire; as his last handler, Springman was first on the list to adopt him, and she happily took him home. Though Springman wished that Dexter could have continued his service, she made it clear at his retirement ceremony that adopting him was one way she could continue to honor him on a daily basis. "To adopt Dexter is the absolute least I could do for him, out of everything he's done for me without question," she said. "I can at least give him a bed to sleep in and all the toys and treats he could ever want."

NOTES

INTRODUCTION

and go places that humans can't. Senior Airman Benjamin Sutton, "More Than a Decade of Service, Military Dog Retires," 366th Fighter Wing Public Affairs, February 1, 2013, http://www.37trw.af.mil/news/story .asp?id=123334715.

as well as force and resource protection. Karen Abeyasekere, "As MWD Retires, Former Handlers Share 'Tails' of Man's Best Friend," 100th Air Refueling Wing Public Affairs, February 27, 2012, https://www.DVIDShub. net/news/84389/mwd-retires-former-handlers-share-tails-mans-best-friend#. VmBThiBVhHx.

the dog can be called back. Cpl. Michelle Reif, "JROTC Students See What All the Bark Is About," DVIDS, March 26, 2015, https://www.DVIDShub. net/news/158160/jrotc-students-see-all-bark-about#.VmmjGiBVhHw.

I put my life in my dog's hands. Lance Cpl. Drew Tech, "Paw Patrol: Military Working Dogs Execute Explosive Detection Training," DVIDS, July 11, 2014, https://www.DVIDShub.net/news/135807/paw-patrol-military-working-dogs-execute-explosive-detection-training#.Vok6XpOANHw.

before he gets sick. Sgt. Marc Loi, "The Last Swearing In: Military Dog Handler Re-enlists Indefinitely," 504th Battlefield Surveillance Brigade, November 17, 2011, https://www.DVIDShub.net/news/80140/last-swearing-military-dog-handler-re-enlists-indefinitely#.VmB5SiBVhHw.

Without one, the other is useless. Sgt. Taryn Hagerman, "All Military Working Dogs Go to Heaven," DVIDS, April 28, 2015, https://www.DVIDShub.net/news/161563/all-military-working-dogs-go-heaven#.VnmSJiBVhHx

then this job isn't for you. Airman 1st Class Christian Clausen, "Let Me Tell You 'bout My Best Friend," DVIDS, November 5, 2014, https://www.DVIDShub.net/news/147037/let-me-tell-you-bout-my-best-friend#.Vn2s-yBVhHw.

to let the dog make mistakes. Airman 1st Class Yash Rojas, "Play a Little, Learn a Lot: MWDs, Handlers Learn to Trust," DVIDS, March 14, 2012, https://www.DVIDShub.net/news/85261/play-little-learn-lot-mwds-handlers-learn-trust#.VpLIFZMrJcA.

fun for the dog . . . and positive. Ibid.

once it's achieved, it's unbreakable. Ibid.

have to be able to deal with. Loi, "The Last Swearing In."

going to get you going. Clausen, "Let Me Tell You 'bout My Best Friend."

get paid to play with dogs all day? Ibid.

1. BASIC TRAINING

day in and day out? Cpl. Charles Santamaria, "'Paws for Reading' Brings Combat Center Families to K-9 Demonstration." DVIDS, July 17, 2014, https://www.DVIDShub.net/news/136440/paws-reading-brings-combat-center-families-k-9-demonstration#.VpLKv5MrJcA.

THE YOUNGEST RECRUIT: DDONJA

Elaine Sanchez, "Breeding Program Turns Puppies into Troops," American Forces Press Service, February 7, 2012, http://archive.defense.gov/news/newsarticle.aspx?id=67089.

FOSTERING LOYALTY: BBELLA

we don't get well-rounded dogs. Elaine Sanchez, "Families Foster Future Military Working Dogs," American Forces Press Service, February 6, 2012, http://archive.defense.gov//news/newsarticle.aspx?ID=67079.

if they were raised in kennels. 2nd Lt. Phil Fountain, "Airmen Open Hearts, Homes to Future Military Working Dogs," 149th Fighter Wing (Texas Air National Guard), November 23, 2014, https://www.DVIDShub.net/news/151000/airmen-open-hearts-homes-future-military-working-dogs#.VmWuCBVhHw.

she cries a blue streak. Sanchez, "Families Foster Future Military Working Dogs."

BASIC TRAINING

Sanchez, "Breeding Program Turns Puppies into Troops."

ADVANCED TRAINING

Randy Roughton, "One Step Away." *Airman,* November 1, 2011, http://airman.dodlive.mil/2011/11/one-step-away/.

SERGEANT GRECO. REPORTING FOR DUTY, SIR!

look on his face. Staff Sgt. Patricia McMurphy, 28th Public Affairs Detachment, "Face of Defense: From Puppy to Police Dog," Defense.gov, July 29, 2015, http://www.defense.gov/News-Article-View/Article/612758/face-of-defense-from-puppy-to-police-dog.

That's their form of currency. Ibid.

won't trust the dog's instincts. Airman Ryan Conroy, "Training Through Discipline; Building MWDs." 31st Fighter Wing Public Affairs, August 29,

2013, http://www.usafe.af.mil/news/story.asp?id=123361448.

I genuinely love my pup. Ibid.

they are ready for anything. Ibid.

2. ACTIVE DUTY

24 hours a day together. Airman 1st Class Betty Chevalier, "From Detection to Relaxation," DVIDS, February 27, 2014, https://www.DVIDShub.net/news/121289/detection-relaxation#.Vm7ffSBVvHw.

to deploy with your best friend. Sgt. Airman 1st Class David Dobrydney, "Military Dog's Desert Life," DVIDS, 379th Air Expeditionary Wing, September 17, 2009, https://www.DVIDShub.net/news/38906/military-dogs-desert-life#.VmW52SBVhHw.

NAVY: BRIT

PO 2nd Class Corwin Colbert, "Face of Defense: Sailor, Working Dog Go to Djibouti," Navy Media Content Services, October 22, 2010, http://archive.defense.gov/news/newsarticle.aspx?id=61377.

AIR FORCE: CIRO

Airman 1st Class David Dobrydney, "Military Dog's Desert Life," 379th Air Expeditionary Wing, September 17, 2009, https://www.DVIDShub.net/news/38906/military-dogs-desert-life#.VmW52SBVhHw.

ARMY: ANDY, ALEX, NIKO, AND LEE: A TEAM EFFORT

Vanessa Villarreal, "Military Working Dog Handlers: 'It's The Best Job Ever,'" www.Army.mil, July 8, 2015, http://www.army.mil/article/151877/Military_working_dog_handlers__It_s_the_best_job_ever_/.

COAST GUARD: NUCKY AND RICKY

a long day patrolling the waters. PO 3rd Class David Micallef, "Nucky's

Tail," USCG District 5 PADET Atlantic City, February 6, 2015, https://www.DVIDShub.net/news/153741/nuckys-tail#.VmYBISBVhHx.

authorization for swim calls. Ibid.

away from the port environment. "K-9 Coast Guard Unites Undergo Special Helicopter Training," KTVU, http://www.ktvu.com/news/31100870-story.

a 60-pound dog that's freaking out. Ibid.

about an inch from my leg. Ibid.

everything was going to be OK. Ibid.

MARINES: WILLY PETE

Cpl. Jeff Drew, "Guardian of Patrols Afghan Dog Fights like Marine," II Marine Expeditionary Force, July 10, 2011, https://www.DVIDShub.net/news/73507/guardian-patrols-afghan-dog-fights-like-marine#. VmB6uSB-VhHw.

3. CONTINUING EDUCATION

what they are tasked to do. Lance Cpl. Abbey Perria, "Dog Teams Use Training as Opportunity to Build Rapport," DVIDS, August 12, 2014. https://www.DVIDShub.net/news/139046/dog-teams-use-training-opportunity-build-rapport#.VovhpJOANHw.

that's what we focus on. Sgt. Airman 1st Class David Dobrydney, "Military Dog's Desert Life," 379th Air Expeditionary Wing, September 17, 2009, https://www.DVIDShub.net/news/38906/military-dogs-desert-life#.Vm-W52SBVhHw.

take care of his daily needs. Senior Airman David Owsianka, "MWD Team Takes Training Downrange," 56th Fighter Wing Public Affairs, May 17, 2013, http://www.luke.af.mil/news/story_print.asp?id=123349039.

Wherever you go, the dog goes. "Bond Like No Other," Stars and Stripes Okinawa, July 2, 2015, http://okinawa.stripes.com/spotlight/daniel-andrzejewski.

which are good distractions for the dogs. Damien Salas, "Military Working Dogs Sniff out Narcotics, Explosives," DVIDS, March 4, 2015, https://www .DVIDSHub.net/news/155921/military-working-dogs-sniff-out-narcotics-ex-plosives#.Vn20riBVhHw.

it is not going to do its job. Lance Cpl. Thomas Mudd, "PMO K9 Division Maintains Readiness with Night Training," Official United States Marine Corps Public Website, January 15, 2015, http://www.marines.mil/News/NewsDisplay/tabid/3258/Article/560211/pmo-k9-division-maintains-readi-ness-with-night-training.aspx.

happy to want to go to work. Master Sgt. Leisa Grant, "Dog Handler's Homegrown Values, Environment Mirror Her K-9 Career," U.S. Air Forces Central Command Public Affairs, May 31, 2013, https://www.DVIDSHub.net/news/107818/dog-handlers-homegrown-values-environment-mirror-her-k-9-career#.VnmRJCBVhHy.

WATER TRAINING: EVERYBODY IN THE POOL!

Cpl. Charles Santamaria, "Dog Days: Aquatics Aggression Class at Base Training Tank," DVIDS, July 17, 2014, https://www.DVIDSHub.net/news/136432/dog-days-aquatics-aggression-class-base-training-tank#.VM-b13iBVhHw.

FLYING

sound of the helicopters and being in air. Staff Sgt. Stephenie Wade, "Pararescueman Train with Army, Military Canines," 455th Air Expeditionary Wing Public Affairs, July 6, 2013, http://www.af.mil/News/ArticleDisplay/tabid/223/Article/108942/pararescueman-train-with-army-military-canines.aspx.

most dog handlers do not get to have. Lance Cpl. Ryan Mains, "Sit, Stay, Rappel: Dogs Fast Rope with Their Handlers," DVIDS, October 20, 2014, https://www.DVIDSHub.net/news/145580/sit-stay-rappel-dogs-fast-rope-with-their-handlers#.VmbsiyBVhHx.

share our knowledge with other Marines. Ibid.

NIGHT VISION

we also do this night training. Mudd, "PMO K9 Division Maintains Readiness with Night Training."

to handle the potential threat. Staff Sgt. Amber Grimm, "K-9 Teams Sniff Out OPFOR During Vigilant Ace 16," DVIDS, November 4, 2015, https://www.DVIDShub.net/news/180819/k-9-teams-sniff-out-opfor-during-vigilant-ace-16#.VovYPpOANHy.

for a longer period of time. Mudd, "PMO K9 Division Maintains Readiness with Night Training."

CHOMP!

and then reinforce it with positive feedback. Cpl. D.J. Wu, "All Bark, All Bite," DVIDS, January 23, 2014, https://www.DVIDShub.net/news/119570/all-bark-all-bite#.VowFgZOANHx.

to become gear dependent. Ibid.

having at least a bite sleeve. "It's Great to Have a Dog in the Fight," April 16, 2009, https://www.DVIDShub.net/news/32446/its-great-have-dog-fight#.VowIZJOANHw.

and knows what to do. Airman 1st Class Jason J. Brown, "Dog Days: ACC Hosts MWD Training Seminar at Langley," DVIDS, July 15, 2010, https://www.DVIDShub.net/news/52885/dog-days-acc-hosts-mwd-training-seminar-langley#.VnmH3SBVhHw.

MAY THE BEST DOG WIN

Senior Airman Scott Saldukas, "Base Hosts DOD Military Working Dog Trials; Navy Handler Claims 'Top Dog' Honors," 47th Flying Training Wing Public Affairs, May 22, 2012, http://www.jbsa.mil/News/News/tabid/11890/

Article/462157/base-hosts-dod-military-working-dog-trials-navy-handler-claims-top-dog-honors.aspx.

4. MOONLIGHTING
LOCAL LAW ENFORCEMENT

Lance Cpl. Tabitha Bartley, "Quantico Working Dogs Assist in Alleged Bomb Threat," Marine Corps Base Quantico, October 17, 2012, https://www.DVIDShub.net/news/96307/quantico-working-dogs-assist-alleged-bomb-threat#.VktC5yBVhHw.

SPECIAL EVENTS

PO 3rd Class Lourmania Stewart, "K-9 Teams Train for Super Bowl 50 Security," DVIDS, December 2, 2015, https://www.DVIDShub.net/news/183350/k-9-teams-train-super-bowl-50-security#.Vo_jMZMrJcA.

PROTECTING VIPS

"Man's Best Friend, Crime's Worst Enemy," DVIDS, November 12, 2015, https://www.DVIDShub.net/news/181832/mans-best-friend-crimes-worst-enemy#.Vn2yUCBVhHw.

EMOTIONAL RESCUE

S. Sgt. Dilia Ayala, "Air Force Theater Hospital 'Unleashes' New Recovery Program for Patients," DVIDS, May 27, 2009, https://www.DVIDShub.net/news/34141/air-force-theater-hospital-unleashes-new-recovery-program-patients#.VktI4yBVhHw.

5: PUBLIC AFFAIRS

regardless of people's reactions. Cpl. Charles Santamaria, "'Paws for Reading' Brings Combat Center Families to K-9 Demonstration," DVIDS, July

17, 2014, https://www.DVIDShub.net/news/136440/paws-reading-brings-combat-center-families-k-9-demonstration#.VnlwJCBVhHz.

better understand what it is we do. Cpl. Aaron Diamant, "Station K-9 Section Showcases Skills for Army Brass," DVIDS, August 8, 2012, https://www.DVIDShub.net/news/92880/station-k-9-section-showcases-skills-army-brass#.VnmBASBVhHw.

READING

Santamaria, "'Paws for Reading' Brings Combat Center Families to K-9 Demonstration."

COMMUNITY DEMONSTRATIONS

showing what our dogs can do. Sgt. Sarah Enos, "Military Showcase All Around Dogs," DVIDS, September 12, 2012, https://www.DVIDShub.net/news/94617/military-showcase-all-around-dogs#.VmmmQiBVhHw.

that is available to them. Sgt. Leejay Lockhart, "Military Working Dog Team Visits Students," 101st Airborne Division Public Affairs, March 14, 2014, https://www.DVIDShub.net/news/122010/military-working-dog-team-visits-students#.VmmkLiBVhHw.

FUTURE HANDLERS

Airman 1st Class R. Alex Durbin, "JBLE Hosts Canadian Air Cadets, Strengthens International Bonds," DVIDS, March 14, 2014, https://www.DVIDShub.net/news/122022/jble-hosts-canadian-air-cadets-strengthens-international-bonds#.VmmjayBVhHw.

HEARTS AND MINDS

Sgt. Mike MacLeod, "Anbar Police Stand Up K-9 Unit," DVIDS, April 23, 2010, https://www.DVIDShub.net/news/48556/anbar-police-stand-up-k-9-unit#.VmBMCCBVhHx.

PREACHING TO THE CHOIR

Cpl. Michelle Reif, "PMO K-9's Entertain WWII Vets," DVIDS, April 27, 2015, https://www.DVIDShub.net/news/161355/pmo-k-9s-entertain-wwii-vets#. VmBDniBVhHw.

6. STRESS RELIEF

It will take you out. Spc. Harold McGill, "Keeping Soldiers in the Game," DVIDS, November 15, 2011, https://www.DVIDShub.net/news/80071/keeping-soldiers-game#. VoBKxJOANHw.

ear muffs and safety goggles. Sgt. Scott Davis, "Staff Sgt. Timmy Combats Stress with Smiles," DVIDS, August 13, 2010, https://www.DVIDShub.net/news/54545/staff-sgt-timmy-combats-stress-with-smiles#.VmB1LSBVhHw.

ZEKE

anything that is possibly bothering them. Spc. Terence Ewings, "Combat Stress Control Soldier, Working Dog Inducted into Order of the Spur," DVIDS, March 23, 2011, https://www.DVIDShub.net/news/67604/combat-stress-control-soldier-working-dog-inducted-into-order-spur#.VoBOSpOANHw.

deal with in this environment. Spc. Darryl Montgomery, "Therapy Dog Visits Spin Boldak," 504th Battlefield Surveillance Brigade, October 8, 2011, https://www.DVIDShub.net/news/78207/therapy-dog-visits-spin-boldak#.VmByBCBVhHw.

MAJOR EDEN

me just going to them. Senior Airman Kayla Newman, "Maj. Eden Brings Major Joy to Service Members," DVIDS, February 10, 2014, https://www.DVIDShub.net/news/120366/maj-eden-brings-major-joy-service-members#.VmBnCiBVhHw.

and how we can help them out. Lt.j.g. Bryan Mitchell, "Therapy Dog Tours Afghanistan," DVIDS, March 15, 2014, https://www.DVIDShub.net/news/122058/therapy-dog-tours-afghanistan#. VmBr0SBVhHw.

how happy it makes them. Newman, "Maj. Eden Brings Major Joy to Service Members."

we're really making a difference. Mitchell, "Therapy Dog Tours Afghanistan."

MAJOR TIMMY

what a rough week it had been. "Dog and Handler Help Relieve Battle Stress for Deployed Soldiers," DVIDS, October 19, 2011, https://www.DVIDShub.net/news/78733/dog-and-handler-help-relieve-battle-stress-deployed-soldiers#.VoE_J5OANHw.

not the everyday norm in Afghanistan. Ibid.

getting some outlet and talking to someone. Tech. Sgt. Vernon Cunningham, "Major Timmy Aids Regional Mental Health Goals," 455th Air Expeditionary Wing, April 25, 2012, https://www.DVIDShub.net/news/87297/major-timmy-aids-regional-mental-health-goals#. VmB0PSBVhHw.

LUGNUT

Jill Swank, "Therapy Goes to the Dogs," Camp Atterbury Public Affairs, August 9, 2011, https://www.DVIDShub.net/news/75087/therapy-goes-dogs#. VmBwfCBVhHw.

7. AT YOUR SERVICE
SHAMUS

Cpl. Lisette Leyva, "Marine's Best Friend," Marine Corps Wounded Warrior Regiment, March 12, 2014, https://www.DVIDShub.net/news/121891/marines-best-friend#.VmmRGiBVhHw.

JAMES

Sgt. 1st Class Jon Cupp, "Warriors Receive Therapy Through Service Dog Training Program," DVIDS, September 8, 2015, https://www.DVIDShub. net/news/175412/warriors-receive-therapy-through-service-dog-training-program#. VmmP7CBVhHw.

PRISON PUPPIES

to do something for somebody else. Lance Cpl. Rebecca Eller, "Bettering Themselves Through Helping Others," Marine Corp Air Station Miramar, January 27, 2012, https://www.DVIDShub.net/news/82947/bettering-themselves-through-helping-others#. VmmRyiBVhHw.

making something good happen. Ibid.

the things that they have done. Sgt. Adam Keith, "Inmates, 'Paws' for a Cause," 19th Public Affairs Detachment, January 28, 2013, https://www. DVIDShub.net/news/101152/inmates-paws-cause#. VpKCaZMrJcB.

and he'll be there. Ibid.

when the dog is around. Ibid.

DINO

Lance Cpl. Angel Serna, "'Man's Best Friend' Is Adopted by Fallen Marine's Family," DVIDS, June 9, 2014, https://www.DVIDShub.net/ news/132585/mans-best-friend-adopted-fallen-marines-family#.VmiKwyB-VhHy.

MUSH!

Sgt. Balinda O'Neal Dresel, "Alaska Guardsman's Kennel Offers Healing to Battle Wounded, Weary," Alaska National Guard Public Affairs, December 24, 2014, https://www.DVIDShub.net/news/151087/alaska-guardsmans-kennel-offers-healing-battle-wounded-weary#. VmXJ7iBVhHw.

ISSAC

Airman 1st Class Tom Brading, "A Warrior's Best Friend," DVIDS, December 2, 2011, https://www.DVIDShub.net/news/80845/warriors-best-friend#.VmmR9SBVhHw.

8. SECOND ACTS

is give them a home. Sgt. James Bunn, "New Lives for Old Dogs," 5th Mobile Public Affairs Detachment, August 6, 2014, https://www.DVIDShub.net/news/138479/new-lives-old-dogs#. VmmknCBVhHw.

the good life of an actual dog. Sgt. Leejay Lockhart, "Soldiers Help Out Teammate with Retirement," DVIDS, September 29, 2014, https://www.DVIDShub.net/news/143556/soldiers-help-out-teammate-with-retirement#. Vmml_iBVhHx.

SATO

Amber Baillie, "Retired Military Working Dog Relieves Stress," U.S. Air Force Academy Public Affairs, May 7, 2015, http://www.retirees.af.mil/news/story.asp?id=123447494.

CARLY

1st Lt. Alexis McGee, "Wounded Warrior Adopts Four-Legged Partner, Friend," Joint Base McGuire-Dix-Lakehurst, September 9, 2013, https://www.DVIDShub.net/news/113314/wounded-warrior-adopts-four-legged-partner-friend#.VmmYQSBVhHw.

IVY

Claudia Feldman, "Marine and His Bomb Dog Reunite," *Houston Chronicle,* February 18, 2014, http://www.houstonchronicle.com/news/article/Marine-and-his-bomb-dog-reunite-5246769.php http://missionk9rescue.org/war-dog-comes-home/

TORA

Airman 1st Class Cary Smith, "Inseparable Bond Continues as Furry Friend Joins the Family," 31st Fighter Wing Public Affairs, August 9, 2015, https://www.DVIDShub.net/news/172586/inseparable-bond-continues-furry-friend-joins-family#.VmmnEyBVhHw.

BERNIE

Cpl. Aaron Diamant, "Station Working Dog Retires After a Lifetime of Service," DVIDS, March 7, 2012, https://www.DVIDShub.net/news/84881/station-working-dog-retires-after-lifetime-service#.VmmlHCBVhHw.

9. STAND DOWN

Airman 1st Class Betty Chevalier, "From Detection to Relaxation," DVIDS, February 27, 2014, https://www.DVIDShub.net/news/121289/detection-relaxation#.VmBPuSBVhHx.

TANJA

Senior Airman Benjamin Sutton, "More Than a Decade of Service, Military Dog Retires," 366th Fighter Wing Public Affairs, February 1, 2013, http://www.37trw.af.mil/news/story.asp?id=123334715.

KOBUS

just an instant bond. Sgt. Taryn Hagerman, "All Military Working Dogs Go to Heaven," DVIDS, April 28, 2015, https://www.DVIDShub.net/news/161563/all-military-working-dogs-go-heaven#.VnmSJiBVhHx.

in such a short amount of time. Spc. Taryn Hagerman, "Ahead of the Pack: Military Working Dog and His Handler to Lead Searches in Afghanistan," DVIDS, June 28, 2013, https://www.DVIDShub.net/news/109470/ahead-pack-military-working-dog-and-his-handler-lead-searches-afghanistan#. VnmWQyBVhHw.

do good things with him. Ibid.

he would go nuts. Hagerman, "All Military Working Dogs Go to Heaven."

I've ever dealt with. Ibid.

have part of him with me. Ibid.

DAYSI

Airman 1st Class Justine Rho, "Final Salute in Honor of MWD Daysi," 502nd Air Base Wing Public Affairs, March 23, 2015, http://www.aetc. af.mil/News/ArticleDisplay/tabid/136/Article/581216/final-salute-in-honor-of-mwd-daysi.aspx.

DIESEL AND DOBRYNYA

for this puppy in Paris. Paul Dallison, "Russia's Puppy Love for France," Politico.eu, December 7, 2015, http://www.politico.eu/article/russia-puppy-dobrynya-replace-police-dog-killed-in-paris-diesel/.

very proud to honour him in this way. "Tragic French Police Dog Diesel to Receive Supreme Honour for Gallantry," People's Dispensary for Sick Animals, December 27, 2015, https://www.pdsa.org.uk/press-office/latest-news/2015/12/22/police-dog-diesel-to-receive-supreme-honour-for-gallantry.

DEXTER

Chevalier, "From Detection to Relaxation."

PHOTO CREDITS

INTRODUCTION

Soldier holding dog: PO 3rd Class Diana Quinlan / U.S. Navy; Soldier sitting with German shepherd: Senior Airman Aubrey White / U.S. Air Force; Soldiers with biting dog: Senior Airman Perry Aston / U.S. Air Force; Soldier with black dog: Airman 1st Class Christian Clausen / U.S. Air Force; Four soldiers holding dogs: Cpl. Joshua Young / U.S. Marine Corps; Soldier and dog with sunglasses: Lance Cpl. Megan Sindelar / U.S. Marine Corps

1. BASIC TRAINING

INTRODUCTION: Man holding puppy: Linda Hosek / DOD; Soldier with puppies: S.Sgt. James Hunter / U.S. Army

THE YOUNGEST RECRUIT: Ddonja: Linda Hosek / DOD

FOSTERING LOYALTY: Bbella: Linda Hosek / DOD

BASIC TRAINING: Brindle dog: Senior M.Sgt. Mike Arellano / U.S. Air National Guard; Big Ears: Senior Airman Melanie Hutto / U.S. Air Force

ADVANCED TRAINING: Tech. Sgt. Bennie J. Davis III / U.S. Air Force; Sergeant Greco. Reporting for Duty, Sir!: S.Sgt. Patricia McMurphy / U.S. Army

2. ACTIVE DUTY

INTRODUCTION: Soldier and dog in profile: Cpl. Reece Lodder / U.S. Marine Corps; Soldier with scope: Airman 1st Class Jeremy L. Mosier / U.S. Air Force

NAVY: Brit: PO 2nd Class Corwin Colbert / U.S. Navy

AIR FORCE: Ciro: Tech. Sgt. Jason Edwards / U.S. Air Force

ARMY: Andy, Alex, Niko, and Lee: A Team Effort — Sgt. 1st Class David Wheeler / U.S. Army

COAST GUARD: Nucky and Ricky: Nucky: PA2 Cynthia Oldham / U.S. Coast Guard; Ricky: ME1 Chris Hartman / U.S. Coast Guard

MARINES: Willy Pete: PO 1st Class Brian Dietrick / U.S. Marines

3. CONTINUING EDUCATION

INTRODUCTION: Dog on Chair: S. Sgt. Marleah Miller / U.S. Air Force; Dog with Box: Maj. Eve Baker / U.S. Marine Corps

WATER TRAINING: EVERYBODY IN THE POOL!: Man with bite suit: Cpl.

Charles Santamaria / U.S. Marine Corps; Dog on shoulders: S. Sgt. Jess Lockoski / U.S. Air Force; Dog being lowered into water: Mass Communication Spc. 2nd Class Corey T. Jones / U.S. Navy

FLYING: S. Sgt. Stephenie Wade / U.S. Air Force; Three dogs: ME1 Chris Hartman / U.S. Coast Guard; Two dogs touching paws: ME1 Chris Hartman / U.S. Coast Guard

NIGHT VISION: Round photo: Cpl. Aaron Diamant / Marine Corps; Dog Police K-9: S. Sgt. Amber Grimm / U.S. Air Force; Green closeup: Spc. Vang Seng Thao / U.S. Army

CHOMP!: Blue suit: PO 1st Class Eric Dietrich / U.S. Navy; Woman with dog: Airman 1st Class Devin Boyer / U.S. Air Force; Man with two dogs: PO 1st Class Eric Dietrich / U.S. Navy

MAY THE BEST DOG WIN: Soldier carrying dog and dragging dummy: Senior Airman Corey Hook / U.S. Air Force; Dog in tunnel: Airman 1st Class Andrew Crawford / U.S. Air Force

4. MOONLIGHTING
INTRODUCTION: Dog with biscuit: Tech. Sgt. John Wiggins / Minnesota National Guard; Dog in kitchen: Damien Salas / U.S. Army

LOCAL LAW ENFORCEMENT: Soldier kneeling with dog: Lance Cpl. Tabitha Bartley / Marine Corps Base Quantico; Dog in orange bleachers: Damien Salas / U.S. Army

SPECIAL EVENTS: Officer on boat: PO 3rd Class Adam Stanton / U.S. Coast Guard; Alcatraz Clipper: PO 2nd Class Barry Bena / U.S. Coast Guard

PROTECTING VIPS: Dog with flag backdrop: Sgt. Brandon Anderson / U.S. Army; Dog at car: Cpl. Michelle Reif / U.S. Marine Corps

EMOTIONAL RESCUE: S. Sgt. Dilia Ayala / U.S. Air Force

5. PUBLIC AFFAIRS

INTRODUCTION: Soldier with dog: S. Sgt. Richard Wrigley / U.S. Army; Smiling soldier holding dog: M. Sgt. April Lapetoda / U.S. Air Force

READING: Cpl. Charles Santamaria / Marine Corps Air Ground Combat Center, Twentynine Palms, California

COMMUNITY DEMONSTRATIONS: Sgt. Sarah E. Enos / U.S. Army / 5th Mobile Public Affairs Detachment

FUTURE HANDLERS: S. Sgt. Katie Gar Ward / U.S. Air Force

HEARTS AND MINDS: Man: Sgt. Mike MacLeod / 1st Brigade Combat Team, 82nd Airborne Division Public Affairs; Girl: Capt. Michael Thompson / 48th Brigade, Georgia National Guard; Soldier with children: Cpl. Reece Lodder / U.S. Marine Corps

PREACHING TO THE CHOIR: Cpl. Michelle Reif / U.S. Marine Corps

6. STRESS RELIEF

INTRODUCTION: Dog with Frisbee: Sgt. Johnathon Jobson / U.S. Army; Dog High Five: Lance Cpl. Elizabeth A. Case / U.S. Marine Corps

ZEKE: Two men: S. Sgt. David Carbajal / U.S. Air Force; Woman: S. Sgt.

David Carbajal / U.S. Air Force; Closeup: Spc. Darryl Montgomery / U.S Army

MAJOR EDEN: Ball: Lt.j.g. Bryan Mitchell / U.S. Air Force; Hobson: Maj. Jared D. Auchey / U.S. Army; Hands: Senior Airman Kayla Newman / U.S. Air Force

MAJOR TIMMY: Woman with ball: Courtesy Photo / U.S. Army; Easter bunny ears: Airman 1st Class Ericka Engblom / U.S. Air Force; Soldier Gomez: Courtesy Photo / U.S. Army

LUGNUT: Jill Swank / Camp Atterbury Public Affairs

7. AT YOUR SERVICE

INTRODUCTION: Dog and man: Kristen Wong / U.S. Marine Corps; Dog with Mohawk: Sgt. Christina Wheeler / U.S. Marine Corps

SHAMUS: Cpl. Lisette Leyva / U.S. Marine Corps

JAMES: Sgt. 1st Class Jon Cupp / U.S. Army

PRISON PUPPIES: Black Lab puppies: Sgt. Adam Keith / U.S. Army; Yellow Lab puppies: Cpl. Isaac Lamberth / U.S. Marine Corps

DINO: Lying down: PO 2nd Class Jonathan David Chandler / U.S. Marine Corps; Family and Bracelet photos: Lance Cpl. Angel Serna / U.S. Marine Corps

MUSH!: Sgt. Balinda O'Neal Dresel / U.S. Army National Guard

ISSAC: S. Sgt. Nicole Mickle / U.S. Air Force

8. SECOND ACTS
INTRODUCTION: Dog on chair: Senior Airman William O'Brien / U.S. Air Force; Handshake: Spc. Matt Kuzara / U.S. Army

SATO: Amber Baillie / U.S. Air Force Academy Public Affairs

CARLY: 1st Lt. Alexis McGee / U.S. Air Force

IVY: Stephen Heath

TORA: Airman 1st Class Cary Smith / U.S. Air Force

BERNIE: Cpl. Aaron Diamant / U.S. Marine Corps

9. STAND DOWN
INTRODUCTION: Dog eating cake: Karen Abeyasekere / 100th Air Refueling Wing Public Affairs; Boris closeup: Sgt. Lori Bilyou / U.S. Army

TANJA: Senior Airman Benjamin Sutton / U.S. Air Force

KOBUS: Selfie: courtesy of Sgt. Holly Moore, 550th Military Working Dog Detachment; Military Fatigues: Spc. Taryn Hagerman / U.S. Army

DAYSI: Playing: Benjamin Faske / U.S. Air Force; Hug and salute: Airman 1st Class Justine Rho / U.S. Air Force

DIESEL: Police Nationale; Dobrynya: © epa european pressphoto agency b.v. / Alamy Stock Photo

ACKNOWLEDGMENTS

Thanks to all of the military journalists and photographers, media professionals, and Public Affairs staff members—officers, enlisted, reservists, and civilians — whose jobs often require them to work under dangerous conditions, all with the sole effort to get the story out about Military Working Dogs and the handlers who work with them.

Eternal thanks be to Superagent, aka Scott Mendel, and Elizabeth Dabbett of Mendel Media Group.

Thanks also to Peter Joseph and Melanie Fried at Thomas Dunne Books / St. Martin's Press, as well as Tom Dunne, Sally Richardson, and the late Matthew Shear, for launching this whole canine / critter trajectory starting with *The Dogs of War*. Thanks also to Laura Clark, Staci Burt, Kimberly Lew, and Sarah Schoof for helping make all my books shine.

"Rogak will warm your heart."

—The Examiner on *Dogs of Courage*

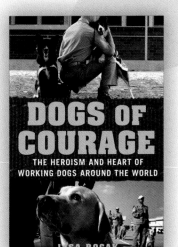